W9-DGL-146

CONTENTS

INTRODUCTION

Reading is a skill, and perhaps the most important skill a child can learn. Although there are a number of methods used for teaching reading, the phonics method is one of the most effective. With the phonics method, the child learns that sounds correspond to alphabet letter symbols. Using these letter sounds, words can be "decoded" and read.

365 Fun Phonics Activities provides fun ways for children to learn letters and the corresponding letter sounds. Children are active learners. Therefore, these phonics activities are designed so the child will be learning by "doing," by using senses, and by asking questions. The book is intended for preschoolers, ages three to six, but children slightly younger and older can benefit from the book's activities as well.

To stimulate the child's interest in reading, you must provide a print-rich environment filled with books, magazines, and newspapers. It is important that the child sees you reading and that you read to the child for pleasure.

Oral communication is also important for language development. Listen to what the child is saying. Talk with him or her as much as possible. With you as a role model, the child will develop good listening and speaking patterns and an interest in learning and reading.

365

PHONICS

Activities

Sandra Fisher
Carole Palmer
Susan Bloom
Joyce Stirniman

CONSULTANT
Elizabeth C. Stull, Ph.D.

ILLUSTRATOR
Anne Kennedy

PUBLICATIONS INTERNATIONAL, LTD.

Elizabeth C. Stull holds a doctorate in early and middle childhood education specializing in curriculum and supervision. She is a visiting assistant professor at Ohio State University-Marion campus, where she teaches language and literacy and children's literature in the master of education program. Dr. Stull has written numerous activity books for teachers, including *Alligators to Zebras: Whole Language Activities for the Primary Grades, Kindergarten Teachers Survival Guide,* and *Multicultural Learning Activities: K-6.*

Sandra Fisher holds a master of education and is assistant professor of elementary education at Kutztown University (PA). She is coordinator of the university's Early Learning Center, a nationally accredited campus laboratory school. She has more than 25 years of classroom experience and has served as vice president of the National Organization of Campus Development Laboratory Schools and as editor of the *NOCDLS Bulletin.*

Carole Palmer holds a master of arts in reading. Previously a first-grade teacher, she currently writes educational material for children, including curriculum for reading programs, spelling series, and phonics projects.

Susan Bloom is a writer and editor with Creative Services Associates, Inc., a publisher of educational materials. She holds a master of arts in English from the University of California-Los Angeles.

Joyce Stirniman is a writer and editor for Creative Services Associates, Inc. She served as field manager for the National Assessment of Education Progress— The Nation's Report Card.

Louis Weber, CEO
Publications International, Ltd.
7373 North Cicero Avenue
Lincolnwood, IL 60712

Manufactured in U.S.A.

8 7 6 5 4 3 2 1

ISBN: 0-7853-4399-7

365 Fun Phonics Activities is divided into seven chapters. Each chapter has activities designated as "easy" (one handprint), "medium" (two handprints), or "challenging" (three handprints). These activity levels are built on the hierarchy of language and reading development.

easy   **medium**   **challenging**

The "easy" level lays the foundation for basic skills; children manipulate objects and call attention to beginning sounds of words. On the "medium" level, the child begins to associate letter symbols and letter sounds through listening skills, letter recognition, and tactile experiences. The activities on the "challenging" level require applying letter symbols to letter sounds and using fine motor skills. Children learn at different rates. Therefore, you may find that the child needs an easier or more challenging activity from one chapter to another.

As you preview these activities, remember that they need not be done in a sequential manner. You should alternate activities, skipping from chapter to chapter, so that the child will have experiences that range from art to cooking to manipulating objects. Read all the materials, the directions, and words of caution for every activity. Some of the activities require *direct* adult supervision because of the materials used (such as scissors) or the nature of the activity (for example, cooking).

As you and the child select an activity, discuss what you are going to do. Talk with the child while he or she is working on a particular project. Be patient, and praise the child as he or she is doing an activity. You may also find it helpful to repeat an activity from time to time. The projects are designed so that they can be enjoyed again and again.

Chapter 1: "Sounds Like Fun." With these

activities, children reinforce their command of beginning letter sounds and listening skills. Rhymes, riddles, and puzzles provide ways to master letter-sound recognition.

Chapter 2: "A B See." Here, the child learns to recognize printed letters. The forms of print used are newspapers, magazines, menus, maps, and alphabet noodles. The activity "Tactile Alphabet" provides an opportunity for the child to create an alphabet book.

Chapter 3: "Eye to Hand." With these activities, the child learns letter recognition and also develops the small muscle coordination necessary for writing. The child manipulates objects, materials, and

writing tools, including pipe cleaners, string, and pens.

Chapter 4: "Word Sense." With these activities, many of which are challenging, children apply their knowledge of letter sounds and recognition to beginning reading. They unscramble letters to form words, observe and read road signs while traveling, and find and read labels at the grocery store.

Chapter 5: "Alphabet Cooking." With the activities in this chapter, children will learn letter sounds while doing two of their favorite things—cooking and eating.

to the home. With these exciting activities, the child learns letters and sounds through an outdoor scavenger hunt, a trip to the zoo, a picnic in the park, and more.

Most of all, have fun with the activities. The more enjoyable the phonics activities are for children, the more they'll want to do them—and the faster they'll learn to read.

Chapter 6: "Alphabet Arts and Crafts." Here, the child uses art materials to explore sounds and letters. Finger painting, bubble blowing, puppet making, and necklace making are among the creative projects.

Chapter 7: "Alphabet Adventures." Phonics activities don't have to be confined

SOUNDS LIKE FUN

B is for *beginning,* and identifying beginning sounds is a big step in learning to read. In Chapter 1 activities, children take that giant step as they listen for the sounds that begin words. Sometimes, as in "Tongue Twister Time," children tell which words begin alike. In other activities, children find objects or think of words beginning with a particular sound. Meanwhile, children do some of their favorite things: mail letters, play cards—even help fold laundry!

 ## ALPHABET TRAIN

Get on the right track with the alphabet train.

WHAT YOU'LL NEED: Boxes of various sizes and shapes, yarn, objects beginning with the different letters of the alphabet

If possible, collect 26 small boxes and one larger box. Leave the open side of each box facing up. Line up the boxes end to end, like the boxcars of a train, then punch a hole in the center of the front and back of each "car." Use yarn to thread through the holes to connect the boxes. Make a knot on each end of the piece of yarn so that the yarn will not slip out.

When all 26 "cars" and one "engine" (the bigger box) are hooked together, write the alphabet on each of the small boxes—one letter per box in alphabetical order. When the train is assembled, ask the child to find some object that begins with each letter and place it in the appropriate "car."

Variation: If you can't find enough boxes, you can assign two or more letters per box.

TONGUE TWISTER TIME

Kids are never too tired to tell tall tongue-twister tales.

Many children have tried the tongue twister "Peter Piper picked a peck of pickled peppers." In this activity, let the child have fun with alliteration and develop a new tongue twister.

It can be challenging to think of a sentence (or phrase) with words that all have the same beginning sound. ABC books, poetry books, and picture books that focus on alliteration can be read to the child. This is an enjoyable exercise and serves as a model.

After the child has developed his or her own tongue twister, see how fast it can be said by both the child and you. Then, test it with the rest of the family.

FINGER FUN

Pointing to pictures helps kids practice their letter sounds.

WHAT YOU'LL NEED: Index cards, old magazines, blunt scissors, glue or clear tape

Play a picture game to help children learn the beginning sound of the letter *F*.

Using pictures cut from old magazines, make several picture cards that show objects whose names begin the same as the word *finger*, such as fence, fox, fish, and fountain. Make additional picture cards using objects that begin with other letters of the alphabet, such as a cat, toaster, bicycle, and so on. Mix the cards.

Point to a picture with your finger. If the picture name begins like the word *finger*, the child should say, "You put your finger on a _____," naming the pictured item. If the picture name does not begin like *finger*, the child should say, *"No fingers here."*

4 SILLY WILLY

Have fun with nonsense rhymes. See how many rhyming words you can use.

Young children get enjoyment from listening to and making up nonsense rhymes.

Begin by giving the child a word, such as *tall.* Ask him or her to think of a rhyming word, such as *ball.* Continue alternating back and forth with the silly rhyming. Even though the word pairs you create may not always make sense, it is important that the child recognizes and responds to the rhyming concept.

ABC—WHAT DO YOU SEE? 5

Children need to be observant to play this game successfully.

Children enjoy solving riddles, and this activity will help a child to become aware of objects in the environment through riddles.

This game may be played in the home or anywhere. Begin by saying: "ABC, what do you see? I see something beginning with *T.*" Have the child solve the riddle by saying something that he or she sees beginning with the letter *T* (for example, *table, teaspoon, tree*). You can give additional clues as needed, such as color, size, shape, function, or location. You can also ask the child to touch the object that he or she identifies. Reverse roles, and have the child choose a letter and start the riddle.

HARD C/SOFT C

6

Is it hard or is it soft? How many C words can you think of?

WHAT YOU'LL NEED: Objects (or pictures of objects) that begin with a *C*

The English language can be difficult for a young child. Some of the letters make a variety of different sounds, so it is important that the child be exposed to them.

Collect objects (or pictures of things) that begin with the letter *C*. The purpose of this activity is for the child to divide these materials into two groups: those with a hard *C* sound, as in *cake,* and ones with a soft *C* sound, as in *celery.* (Sample objects: cup, cookies, ceiling, carrot, circle.)

7

LISTEN CAREFULLY

One word in a group is not like the others. Which is it?

Select a letter of the alphabet, and think of some words that begin with the sound of that same letter. Tell the child that you will be saying three words—two words that begin with the same sound and one word that is different. Say the three words—for example, *cat, ball, bird.* Have the child listen carefully and then tell you which word begins with the different letter sound.

Variation: To make this activity more challenging, say four or five words with the same beginning letter sound and one that is different. You can also reverse roles and have the child think of words that begin similarly and differently.

8 HEART PUZZLE

Take time to solve this puzzle, and mend a broken heart.

WHAT YOU'LL NEED: Lightweight cardboard, marker, blunt scissors

Make a big heart shape on lightweight cardboard, and write the letters *H* and *h* on it in as large a size as possible. Cut the heart into several puzzle-shaped pieces. The child takes the puzzle pieces and puts the puzzle together so that a heart is formed and the letters *H* and *h* are formed. The letters assist the child in assembling the heart puzzle and also in associating the *H* sound with the word *heart*.

SUITCASE SPECIALS 9

Packing for a trip? These suitcase specials are a must.

WHAT YOU'LL NEED: Suitcase, objects that begin with the letter *S*

Planning and going on a trip is an enjoyable experience for most children.

The task in this activity is for the child to find things in the home that begin with the letter *S* that he or she could pack in a suitcase. Items might include socks, sandals, soap, a swimsuit, or a sweater. See what items the child selects. You may have forgotten one of those items on your list.

10 PICTURE DICTIONARY

Make a special book for a special person.

WHAT YOU'LL NEED: Old magazines, 26 sheets of 8½″ × 11″ construction paper of various colors, blunt scissors, glue or clear tape, marker, hole puncher, yarn

Have the child design a "picture dictionary" filled with pictures of things that are of interest to him or her. For example, if the child likes sports, use several old sports magazines for this project.

Write both the capital and lowercase form of one letter of the alphabet in the upper right corner of each of the 26 sheets of construction paper. Give the child an old magazine and blunt scissors, and ask him or her to look for and cut out pictures of things that begin with each letter of the alphabet. Help the child glue or tape a picture on the correct letter page. When all or most of the pages have pictures on them, help the child make a front and back cover. Punch holes on the left side of each page, then bind the pages with yarn.

PHONICS FUN FACT

The most widely used letters in written English are
e, t, a, o, i, n, s, r, h, and *l.*

BUBBLE BABBLE

11

Blow some bubbles, and practice the B sound.

WHAT YOU'LL NEED: Liquid soap, water, large plastic container, drinking straw

Use bubble-blowing to help the child practice beginning sounds.

Make a bubble solution by pouring soap and water into the container, using ¼ cup of soap to one quart of water. Invite the child to blow bubbles with the straw. Each time he or she blows a bubble, say a word. Have the child say a word that begins with the same sound.

LET THE SUN SHINE

12

Follow the winding path, and review the letter S.

WHAT YOU'LL NEED: Construction paper, pen, crayons or markers, blunt scissors, glue, poster board, die and markers from board game

Construct your own board game to practice the beginning sound of the letter *S*.

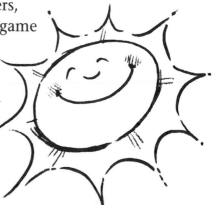

Draw 10 to 15 circles, each with a diameter of about 1½", on construction paper. Ask the child to decorate these "suns" with crayons or markers. Cut them out and paste them on a piece of poster board to form an *S*-shaped path.

Play a game by taking turns moving markers along the path according to the roll of the die. Each player must say a word that begins like the word *sun* in order to leave his or her marker on a circle. The game ends when one player reaches the end of the path.

SNAP LETTERS

Instead of using those clothespins on a clothesline, try snapping them on pictures.

WHAT YOU'LL NEED: Eight magazine pictures, lightweight cardboard, compass, glue or clear tape, eight clothespins, blunt scissors, felt-tip pen

This activity reinforces eight different beginning sounds.

Take a piece of lightweight cardboard and, using a compass, draw and cut out a circle approximately 8″ wide. Use the pen to divide the circle into eight equal sections, as if it were a pie. Next, cut out pictures of familiar objects from a magazine (for example, ball, pen, fish, dog, carrot, hat, shoe, apple). Make sure that each picture is small enough to fit into one section of the circle and that no two objects begin with the same letter. Glue or tape the pictures in place.

On the opening end of each snap clothespin, write a letter that matches the first letter of the object in each picture (in our example, the letters *B, P, F, D, C, H, S,* and *A*). Ask the child to take each lettered clothespin and snap it onto the section of the circle that has an object whose first letter begins with the same letter. Continue until all the letter matches are made.

If the child has difficulty with certain letters, focus on those letters the next time you do this activity. (Hint: You can use the back of the circle to repeat this activity with a new set of letters.)

14 LOOK AT ME

Watch what happens when you talk into a mirror.

WHAT YOU'LL NEED: Mirror

Mirrors are fascinating to children. This activity allows them to see what lip and mouth movements occur when different words are spoken.

Tell the child various words and have him or her repeat them while looking in a mirror (for example, *dog* for a *D* sound, *button* for a *B* sound, *milk* for an *M* sound, *tooth* for a *T* sound, *pat* for a *P* sound, and so on). As each word is said, ask the child if his or her lips touched (as when saying words that begin with *B, M,* and *P*). And where was "Mr. Tongue?" Was he touching the front teeth, on the roof of the mouth, or hiding inside?

Ask the child to think of other words that begin with a particular letter and say them to the mirror, seeing if his or her mouth formations are the same for each letter sound.

I SPY 15

Spy an object, and see who can "detect" it.

Play an "I Spy" game by giving clues that include beginning sounds. For example: "I spy something white; it is in the kitchen; it begins like the word *rabbit*." After the child answers correctly (refrigerator), give clues for another object.

LETTER RIDDLES

16

Just a few minutes to spare? Try a letter-riddle game.

While traveling, shopping, or during spare time, play a riddle game that begins, for example, by saying: "I am thinking of the letter that has the beginning sound of *ball*. What letter is it?"

This activity provides many opportunities for riddles. A more challenging approach to the riddle concept is to present a series of clues. For example: "I am thinking of something that begins with a *B*." Allow the child to guess the answer between each successive clue. Continue with more clues: "I am thinking of something that is round; I am thinking of something that goes up very high and may be different colors; I am thinking of something that bounces."

Keep giving clues until the child guesses the object in mind. For a further variation, reverse roles and have the child give the clues. This activity helps develop the child's thinking skills as you progress from general to specific clues.

17

MAIL CALL

All the mail starts with the letter M in this make-believe mailbox activity.

WHAT YOU'LL NEED: Shoe box, old magazines, blunt scissors

Help the child practice recognizing the beginning sound of the letter *M*. Print a large *M* for *mailbox* on the shoe box. Then invite the child to look through magazines for pictures of objects whose names begin with *M*. Help the child cut out the pictures and "mail" them by putting them into the *M* box.

18 — APRON OR APPLE

Here is a challenge to determine if A *words are long or short sounds.*

WHAT YOU'LL NEED: Old catalog, blunt scissors, apron, apple

Old catalogs are good sources for pictures of specific objects. Find some that the child can use for this activity.

Give the child an apron. Ask what it is and what beginning sound he or she hears when saying the word *apron*. In this case, *apron* says its name with a long *A* sound. Then give the child an apple and ask what beginning sound is heard when saying *apple* (the short *A* sound). Give the child a catalog to find things that have long *A* sounds (for example, alien, ape, angel) and short *A* sounds (ant, ax, animal). If the object has a long *A* sound, place it by the apron, and if it has a short *A* sound, place it by the apple.

BOUNCING WORDS — 19

Try bouncing words. It can be more fun than using a ball.

Whenever you have a few minutes, whether you're at home or traveling in the car, try this quick activity involving "bouncing" words from one to another.

Say a word, such as *ball*. The child then says a word that begins with the same first letter, such as *bat*. Continue bouncing new words back and forth to each other until neither of you can think of any more words. Then try a new letter. You can also have someone keep count to see how many words you come up with for each letter.

ALPHABET SONG

20

*An old song is a great way to begin the day—
and learn the alphabet.*

Teach the child the "Alphabet Song":

"A, B, C, D, E, F, G,

H, I, J, K, L, M, N, O, P,

Q, R, S,

T, U, V,

W, X,

Y, and Z.

Now I know my ABCs,

Tell me what you think of me."

By singing this song, the child learns rhyming sounds and the sounds of the letters, at the same time developing a frame of reference for alphabetical order.

For a variation, write the letters of the alphabet on a sheet of paper, and ask the child to point to each letter while singing. You can also record the child singing on a cassette tape that can be played again and again. For a second verse, replace the last line above with: "Won't you come and sing with me?"

RIDDLE TIME

What appears once in a minute,
Once in a blue moon,
Yet never in one hundred years?
(The letter *M*)

21 — ALL EYES AND EARS

Take a close look around the room to find rhyming objects.

WHAT YOU'LL NEED: Collection of objects that can be easily rhymed

In this activity, use objects found in the home to help the child become accustomed to rhyming words.

Show the child an object found in the home (for example, a bat) and have him or her tell you what the object is and then think of a word that rhymes with it. Compare and discuss the difference between the object you chose and the rhyming word selected by the child.

A CLOSE LOOK — 22

A picture is worth a thousand words. What do you see?

WHAT YOU'LL NEED: Detailed ABC picture books

A beginning reader needs to develop the skill of observing and interpreting pictures. ABC books can help because they have illustrations that aid the child's understanding of the relationship between letters and their sounds. Some pages have one word, some have rhyming text, and some use alliteration (two or more words in a row that begin with the same letter sound). These books are useful because they help develop the foundations of phonics. At the same time, they are visually stimulating, helping to maintain a child's attention.

Examine a variety of ABC picture books, then ask the child to take a close look at one of them. Encourage the child to observe as much detail as possible. Next, select just one page and say the word for an item depicted there. The child then needs to find something else on that page that begins with the same letter as the word you said. Alternate turns, paying attention to the letters and sounds as you go through the letters from *A* to *Z*.

LETTER FOR THE DAY

23

*Check your calendar to find out what
special letter day it is.*

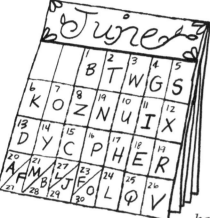

WHAT YOU'LL NEED: Calendar

Not sure what to do, say, wear, or eat on a particular day?
Let this activity help you.

You will need a calendar. Ask the child to randomly pick a
letter of the alphabet for each square that represents a day of
the month. Each night, ask the child to think of things that
could be done the next day beginning with that particular
letter. Using the letter *B* for an example, you could *bounce* a
ball, *bake*, or *blow bubbles*. You could also eat *butter*, *bread*, or a
banana, or wear something *blue*, *brown*, or *black*. Encourage the
child to say all the *B* words he or she can think of. Have fun!

24

THUMBS-UP

Every kid can be a critic and vote "thumbs-up" for U *words.*

Use hand motions to emphasize words that begin with the letter *U.*

Have the child demonstrate the gestures for "thumbs-up" and
"thumbs-down." Explain that when you say a word, he or she
should show thumbs-up if the word begins with the letter *U* or
point thumbs-down if it does not. Words to use might include
apple, *desk*, *ugly*, *under*, *off*, and *umbrella*.

TO RHYME OR NOT TO RHYME

Here's a rhyming game that helps a child develop important language skills.

Being able to hear different sounds in a series of words is an important skill that can be developed in young children.

First explain what a rhyme is. Use a series of two words that sound alike, such as *bat* and *cat* or *dog* and *log*. Once that concept is clear, say three words—two that rhyme and one that does not, such as *bat, cat, mop*. Ask the child to identify the word that doesn't rhyme. (Change the order of words occasionally so that the nonrhyming word isn't always the last word in the group.)

Next, try saying four words—three words that rhyme and one word that doesn't, in any order (for example, *tree, bird, free, key*)—and ask the child if he or she can identify the word that doesn't rhyme. If the child is having difficulty picking the nonrhyming word, have him or her repeat all four words. If the child has trouble recalling all of the words, repeat the list yourself.

PHONICS FUN FACT

The Greeks were the first people to form and to use a true alphabet. The English word *alphabet* is composed of the first two letters of the Greek alphabet, *alpha* and *beta*.

DUCK, DUCK, GRAY DUCK!

Using a traditional game in a new way encourages children to learn.

This adaptation of a traditional game focuses on the beginning sound of the letter *D*.

Invite several family members or friends to sit in a circle on the floor with you and the child. One player walks around the outside of the circle and taps each player, saying "Duck." He or she then stops behind one player and says, "Gray Duck." That player must say a word that begins like the word *duck*, at which point he or she becomes the player who walks around the circle and chooses a "Gray Duck."

ANIMAL SOUNDS

Who says animals can't talk? Listen carefully to what they are saying.

Exposing a child to the sounds that animals make is another way for him or her to be able to identify the sounds of different letters.

"Moooo"

Make a sound that an animal makes, such as "moo." Ask the child to tell you the first letter of that sound. Continue with other animal sounds, having the child identify the beginning letter of each one. Reverse roles. Other sounds you can use: quack, tweet, meow, baa, hee-haw, woof.

Variation: Sing "Old MacDonald Had a Farm" to reinforce the animal sounds. If you have any of the interactive books that have recorded animal sounds, you can play those with the child as well.

RHYME TIME

28

It's time to rhyme with mixtures of pictures.

WHAT YOU'LL NEED: Magazines, index cards, blunt scissors, glue or clear tape

Rhyming words help a child develop listening skills by allowing him or her to compare different letter sounds.

Look through several magazines to find pairs of images that rhyme—for example, a fox and a box, a tree and a key, a hat and a cat, and so on. Glue or tape one picture on each index card, making four or five rhyming pairs of cards. Mix up the cards and place them on the table. Ask the child to identify the item on each card. This will prevent any misnaming of the objects. Next, tell the child to find two pictures that rhyme and place them together. When the child is finished, have him or her recite the pairs of rhyming words.

29 # RECORDING STAR

Every child will feel like a "star" hearing his or her own voice on a tape recorder.

WHAT YOU'LL NEED: Tape recorder

Tape-recording helps reinforce recognition of beginning sounds by using the child's own voice.

Say a simple sentence that includes two words that begin alike. For example, "Mom put the *jelly* in the *jar*." Turn the tape recorder on, and have the child repeat the sentence, then say the two words that begin alike. Play the recording for the child. Then continue with new sentences.

30 — A GORGEOUS GIFT

A surprise awaits you when you open this gorgeous gift.

WHAT YOU'LL NEED: Box, ribbon, gift item that begins with the letter *G*

People enjoy giving gifts almost as much as they enjoy receiving them. This activity lets the child select a gift to give to you, making the exercise an educational experience as well.

Give the child a box. Ask him or her to search in or around the home for a special item that begins with the letter *G* to serve as a gift for you (for example, gloves, golf balls, a game, grapes, etc.). Ask the child to put the object in the box without telling or showing you what it is. Have the child use ribbon to tie around the box (if he or she knows how to do so). When the child gives you the gift, he or she must provide you with clues (for example, "you use this outside") until you are able to guess what it is. After you guess what the item is, review all the *G* words talked about in this activity (*gift, give, guess,* etc.).

SOUND SORT

Sorting pictures by beginning sounds is great exercise for hands and minds.

WHAT YOU'LL NEED: Two shoe boxes, old magazines, blunt scissors, tape

Sorting pictures can help children practice identifying letter sounds.

Cut out pictures of objects out of old magazines. Tape a picture of an object (for example, a table) on the front of one of the shoe boxes. Have the child look through the other pictures you have cut out and put into the box the pictures whose names begin with the same sound as the word *table*. Then change the picture on the first box and tape a picture on the second box. Have the child sort through the pictures again, putting them into the two boxes according to beginning sounds.

This activity will work best if you find three or more pictures of things that begin with the same letter. For a variation, have the child sort actual objects.

ALPHABET WORD CHALLENGE

How many words can you think of that begin with a certain letter?

WHAT YOU'LL NEED: Alphabet cards

After the child learns the alphabet and its letter sounds, this activity will provide a good review of letters and their sounds.

Show the child a letter of the alphabet. The challenge is for the child to name as many things as he or she can beginning with that letter. If a letter has different sounds (for example, the letter *C*, which can be hard or soft), encourage the child to use words with all the possible sounds of that particular letter.

PLEASE DROP IN

While kids drop clothespins into a bottle, they learn different letter sounds.

WHAT YOU'LL NEED: Plastic container (such as a one-gallon milk container) with the top cut off, plastic clothespins

Have the child practice the letter *P* sound by playing a variation of an old party favorite. Put the container on the floor, and have the child stand an arm's length away from it. Give the child five clothespins and instruct him or her to stand straight while attempting to drop each clothespin into the container. After dropping a pin into the container, the child must say a word that begins with *P*.

After the child drops the five clothespins, start over using a new word with a different first letter, such as *milk*, *bottle*, or *container*.

PHONICS FUN FACT

Letters *I*, *T*, *L*, and *X* are the easiest letters to make.

PHONICS GO FISH

34

Do you have a picture of something that begins like the word sun? *Go fish!*

WHAT YOU'LL NEED: 10 index cards, 10 pictures of objects cut from magazines, blunt scissors, glue or clear tape

The card game "Go Fish" is ideal for identifying words with the same beginning sounds.

Cut 10 pictures from magazines and attach each one to an index card. Each picture name should have the same beginning sound as another picture name; for example, *bed/boy, cookie/car, lamp/lake, house/horse, roof/refrigerator.*

Shuffle the cards, then deal five cards to the child and five to yourself. First, lay down any pairs with matching sounds that either of you have. Then take turns asking each other for a card that will make a pair when combined with a card you already have. For example, "Do you have a picture whose name begins like *boy?*"

PHONICS FUN FACT

English is a growing language. At the turn of the century, words were added at the rate of 1000 per year. Now, the increase is closer to 15,000 to 20,000 words per year. In 1987, the *Random House Dictionary* included 50,000 words that did not exist 21 years earlier and 75,000 new definitions of old words.

HIDDEN HANDS

35

Hands can't talk, but they can still tell you things.

WHAT YOU'LL NEED: Box, collection of objects to feel

The five senses play a vital role in the life of a child. In this activity, the sense of touch is used.

To introduce this activity, show the child five objects (for example, apple, ball, feather, ribbon, and sock), and have the child say what the objects are. After the objects are properly identified, cut a hole in the box that is large enough for the child's hand to fit through. Place the objects inside the box. Then ask the child to reach inside, grasp an object, and describe what he or she is holding while saying what the beginning letter sound of the object is.

Variation: Place five objects in the box without showing them to the child. Then ask him or her to feel, describe, name, and identify the beginning letter sound of the object.

36

WASH-DAY WORDS

Kids can learn beginning sounds by folding towels and T-shirts.

WHAT YOU'LL NEED: Clean laundry

Make helping out around the house a game of matching beginning sounds. As you and the child fold and sort clean laundry, have the child name each item and then say another word that begins with the same sound: *socks/sun, jeans/jump, towel/toy.*

SHOW TIME

▼▼▼▼▼▼▼▼▼▼▼▼▼▼▼▼▼▼▼▼▼▼▼▼▼▼▼▼▼▼▼

37

Television is not just for couch potatoes. The TV can be a tool for sharpening listening skills.

WHAT YOU'LL NEED: Television, videocassette of children's movie or TV show (optional)

Encourage the child to watch television with a phonics purpose: listening for beginning sounds.

Before the child watches a program or video, ask him or her to listen for words that begin with a particular sound. For example, while watching *The Lion King,* the child might listen for words that begin like *lion.* Encourage the child to say each *L* word aloud.

38

WIGGLE WORMS

●●●●●●●●●●●●●●●●●●●●●●●●●●●●●●●●●●

Worms can do wonders when you want to try the letter W sound.

WHAT YOU'LL NEED: Pipe cleaner, pencil

This art activity can be used to draw attention to the beginning sound of the letter *W.*

Show the child how to make a "worm" by winding a pipe cleaner around a pencil. Slide the "worm" off the pencil, and invite the child to make the worm crawl around as you count to 10. Before you reach 10, the child must say a word that begins like *worm.*

39 PILLOWCASE PICKS

A prize awaits the participant when the pillowcase is filled.

WHAT YOU'LL NEED: Pillowcase, objects that begin with the letter *P*

In addition to a pillow, have the child find other objects in your home that begin with the letter *P*.

Show the child a pillowcase. Ask what goes inside a pillowcase. The child should respond with "pillow." Ask the child to make the sound of the *P* in the word *pillowcase*. Give the child the pillowcase and have him or her find and place different objects that begin with the letter *P* inside it (for example, pen, pencil, piece of popcorn, paintbrush).

When the child has collected every item he or she could identify, put them on the table and review the items. As you are talking with the child, use as many *P* words in your conversation as you can. When you are finished, give the child a prize of a Popsicle, peanuts, or a pear (or anything else that begins with the letter *P*) for the successful completion of this activity.

DRESS FOR SUCCESS 40

Clothes make the child—or at least the child's phonics knowledge—in this start-the-day activity.

WHAT YOU'LL NEED: Several items of clothing

As the child gets dressed in the morning, play a beginning-sound guessing game using at least three items of his or her clothing.

Start this way: "Now it's time to put on something that begins like the word *party*." (Answer: pants.) Have the child guess each piece of clothing before putting it on. This game can also be played at bedtime using a nightgown, pajamas, robe, and slippers.

PICK A PUMPKIN

You don't have to wait for autumn to create an educational pumpkin patch.

WHAT YOU'LL NEED: Orange construction paper, pencil, blunt scissors

Make learning the sound of the letter *P* fun by creating a pumpkin patch.

Help the child draw and cut out several pumpkins from orange construction paper. Place the pumpkins around the room. Ask the child to gather pumpkins from the "patch" by saying a word that begins like *pumpkin* each time he or she picks up a pumpkin.

SIMON SAYS SOUND ALIKE

Simon says that the words listening *and* learning *start alike.*

Play a version of "Simon Says" that focuses on beginning sounds in words. If "Simon" makes a correct statement, the child should follow the given directions. If "Simon" makes an incorrect statement, the child should not.

For example, if you say, "Simon says *finger* and *football* begin alike; wiggle your finger," the child should follow the directions and wiggle his or her finger. However, if you say, "Simon says *tongue* and *nose* begin alike; stick out your tongue," the child should not follow the directions because the statement is incorrect.

Stick out your tongue!

Simon

TONGUE TWISTER TOUGHIES

43

Kids can catch on to consonants while considering catchy quips.

Tongue twisters are ideal for recognizing words that begin with the same sound. Say one of the following tongue twisters slowly, and repeat it several times. Ask the child to repeat the words that begin with the same sound.

Peter Piper picked a peck of pickled peppers.

Silly Sara sang a song at sunset.

Rubber baby buggy bumpers.

A big black bug bit a big brown bear.

The wild wolf wanders the wintry woods.

Round and round the rugged rocks, the ragged rascal ran.

44

IN-BASKET

A-tisket, a-tasket—here's a beginning-sound basket!

WHAT YOU'LL NEED: Index cards, marker or pen, small basket

Here's an "office" activity that encourages children to practice letter sounds.

Make letter cards by writing a large letter (for example, *B, D, G, S,* and *T*) on each of several index cards. Give the child one card (for instance, the letter *B*) and have him or her say a word that begins with the same letter (such as *bed*). After giving a word with the correct beginning sound, the child drops the card into the "in-basket." If the child's word does not have the correct first-letter sound, put the card aside and continue with the other cards.

BALL-TOSS RHYMES

45

Test a child's verbal skills with a bouncing rubber ball.

WHAT YOU'LL NEED: Rubber ball

Rhyming words are an effective way for a child to develop listening skills and acquire the ability to make new words.

Think of a simple rhyming word, such as *hat*. As you throw, bounce, or roll the ball to the child, say the word *hat*. The child, after receiving the ball, is to say a rhyming word (for example, *cat, fat, mat, sat, rat, pat*) before he or she returns the ball to you. Repeat transferring the ball back and forth and saying a rhyming word. If the child cannot think of a new word, have him or her say *hat*. Then it's up to you to give a rhyming word.

46

TELL ME A STORY

Here's one way to get applause whenever you tell a story.

Use verbal storytelling to practice listening for beginning sounds. Ask the child to listen for words that begin with a particular sound (such as the *B* sound) as you tell a simple story. For example: "I went outside and took my *bat*. I picked up a *ball*. I ran around the *bases*." Have the child clap each time he or she hears a word that begins with the chosen sound and then repeat the word.

47 BATTER UP

See if students of beginning sounds can hit a home run.

WHAT YOU'LL NEED: Index cards, old magazines, glue or clear tape, blunt scissors

Sports lovers can play baseball as they learn beginning sounds.

Make picture cards by gluing or taping pictures of simple objects onto index cards. Place the pictures around the room or yard in a baseball-diamond pattern. Have the child walk or run from home plate to first base. At first base, ask him or her to name the object on the picture card and say a word that has the same beginning sound. If the child's word has the correct beginning sound, he or she goes on to the next base.

Let the child continue until he or she reaches home plate and scores a "home run." Play the game again using new picture cards, or actual sports items.

HELLO/GOOD-BYE 48

Hello, horse; good-bye goat!

In this activity, the child is asked to recognize the beginning sounds *G* and *H*. Say a series of words that begin with *H* and *G*, such as *hat, girl, head, horse, gate, garden, hand, goat,* and *house*. Have the child say "hello" each time you say a word that begins with *H* and "good-bye" each time you say a word that begins with *G*.

RED RAKES, PURPLE PIGS

49

Here's a colorful way to learn beginning letter sounds.

WHAT YOU'LL NEED: Paper, old magazines, blunt scissors, crayons or colored markers

Use children's knowledge of colors to help them learn beginning sounds.

First, help the child make a color wheel. Draw a circle and divide it into six sections, like a pie. Color the sections in this order: red, purple, blue, green, yellow, orange. Make picture cards by cutting out a picture whose name has the same beginning sound as each color word—for example, a rake for red, a pig for purple, a blanket for blue, grass for green, yarn for yellow, and an orchestra for orange.

Ask the child to name each color on the wheel and then place the picture with the same beginning sound next to it. Children who are more advanced can find their own matching pictures.

50

JACK-IN-THE-BOX

Children will jump for joy when they learn the letter J.

Play an active game that emphasizes the beginning sound *J*.

Ask the child to demonstrate the action of a jack-in-the-box. Say the words *jump* and *jack*. Have the child say additional words that begin with the *J* sound. Explain that you will say a word. If it begins with the *J* sound, like *jack-in-the-box*, the child jumps up. If it does not begin with the *J* sound, the child stays "in the box." Begin with the words *jar, sand, tree, jet, jelly, box, jeep,* and *pear.*

51 LETTER LONDON BRIDGE

London Bridge is falling down—unless kids can identify beginning sounds.

WHAT YOU'LL NEED: Index cards, old magazines, blunt scissors, glue or clear tape

Here's a new slant on an old singing game that will help children practice letter sounds.

Make picture cards by cutting out pictures of simple objects and pasting or taping them onto index cards. To play the game, sing "London Bridge Is Falling Down" with a small group of children. The players walk one by one through the bridge formed by two other players. When the song ends, the player inside the bridge is "caught." In order to be "released," he or she looks at a picture card, identifies it, and then gives a word with the same first-letter sound as the object in the picture.

52 T PARTY

This activity will definitely put the T *into tea party.*

WHAT YOU'LL NEED: Dishes, table, tablecloth, teacups, teaspoons, straws or Popsicle sticks, clay, small flowerpot or bowl, construction paper, marker or pen, blunt scissors, glue

Hold a real or "pretend" tea party that includes many foods and objects whose names have the beginning sound *T*.

With the child's help, identify tea-party items whose names begin with the *T* sound. Discuss each step with the child: Set the table with a tablecloth, dishes, teacups, and teaspoons.

Have the child create a centerpiece by putting a letter *T* made out of drinking straws or Popsicle sticks in a piece of clay placed in a small flowerpot or bowl. Next, make "tulips" by drawing tulip-blossom shapes on various colors of construction paper, cutting them out, and gluing them to the Popsicle sticks or straws.

Ask the child to help create the menu and serve some of the following real or pretend foods: tea, toast, tuna, and tarts.

RIDDLE TIME

What happens when ghosts fall down?
(They get boo-boos.)

53 ALPHABET BOUQUET

What could be more beautiful? A bouquet with a flower for each letter of the alphabet.

WHAT YOU'LL NEED: Flowers—one each of as many different varieties as possible

From a garden or flower market, such as the one at a grocery store, let the child choose and pick (or buy) one each of several different types of flowers, such as a rose, carnation, daisy, tulip, daffodil, and lily. As the child chooses a flower, name it. The child then has to say a word with the same beginning sound as the flower's name.

Continue identifying flower names and words with the same beginning sounds as you take the bouquet home and while you arrange the flowers for display. Do so until the child can identify each flower name, as well as other words with the same beginning sound.

WASH, RINSE, DRY 54

Here's an alphabet game to make those tiresome bath time tasks lots of fun.

WHAT YOU'LL NEED: Bathtub, water, washcloth, soap, towel

At bath time, try this beginning-sound chanting game.

Start with the word *wash.* As the child washes each arm, each leg, torso, and face with soap and cloth, he or she chants, "w-w-wash my arms, w-w-wash my legs," and so on for each body part. Repeat the activity with the word *rinse* ("r-r-rinse") as the child rinses each body part. Finally, use the word *dry* ("d-d-dry") as the child dries each body part.

THE MISSING D'S

55

Become a detective and find the missing D's.

WHAT YOU'LL NEED: Magnifying glass, household items that begin with the letter *D*

Role-playing is an important way for a child to learn, and pretending to be a detective can be challenging and exciting.

Give the child a magnifying glass. The "detective" searches the home for things that begin with the letter *D*. Have the child collect the *D* things in a dishpan. (Hints: doll, stuffed dog, dime, dish, dice, domino, drum, diaper.)

If the child has a yellow rain slicker, it could be used as an additional prop to make him or her look like detective Dick Tracy.

56 # DISH-WASHING TIME

Discuss D words while you do the dishes.

WHAT YOU'LL NEED: New kitchen sponges, blunt scissors, glue, construction paper, dirty dishes

The child will learn all about the letter *D* in this kitchen activity.

Cut up a new kitchen sponge into strips about one inch wide. Help the child glue them onto construction paper to make three-dimensional versions of the letters *D* and *d*. Display the letters in the kitchen near the sink. Emphasize the *D* sound as the child helps you wash dishes. Discuss the process using a variety of *D* words: *dirty dishes, draining, drying, dishwasher, dishrag,* and *dish towel*.

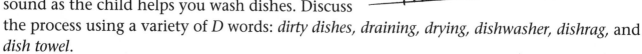

CIRCLE KITES

Tell kids to go fly a kite—and learn about the letter **K.**

WHAT YOU'LL NEED: Kraft paper, blunt scissors, crayons, tissue paper or crepe paper, glue or clear tape, string

This activity helps children become familiar with *K*, a rarely used beginning letter.

Cut a circle with a diameter of about 12″ to 18″ from the kraft paper. Ask the child to write the upper- and lowercase letter *K* on the paper circle, then identify three things that begin with the *K* sound—for example, a kangaroo, key, and kettle.

Make eight or 10 streamers, approximately 1″ × 18″, out of colorful tissue paper or crepe paper. Help the child glue or tape the ends of the streamers around the edge of the paper circle. Next, punch two small holes in the center of the kite, then put a string approximately 24″ long through the holes, tying it so that the string is on the opposite side of the kite from the streamers. As the child runs outside, pulling the kite with the string, the streamers will float behind.

RIDDLE TIME

What two letters did Mother Hubbard find in her cupboard? (MT)

58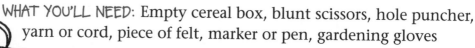

LITTER PATROL

Kids can be good citizens while they learn about the letter L.

WHAT YOU'LL NEED: Empty cereal box, blunt scissors, hole puncher, yarn or cord, piece of felt, marker or pen, gardening gloves

Children can spruce up the neighborhood and learn the letter *L* at the same time.

Make a litter collector by cutting the top off an empty cereal box. Punch a hole in each side of the box near the top, then put the yarn or cord through the holes. Tie the two ends together to form a loop.

On a piece of felt, draw a two-dimensional capital letter *L*. Cut out the letter and paste it on the litter collector. Explain to the child that *L* stands for the word *litter*.

As you walk through the neighborhood or a park, have the child put on gardening gloves and pick up paper, wrappers, and other litter that you find along the way, putting them in the litter collector. Dispose of this in a proper container to show the child where litter belongs.

NURSERY RHYMES

59

Where did Jack and Jill go, and what happened to Humpty Dumpty? Fill in the rhyming words.

Simple nursery rhymes help a child acquire rhyming and listening skills.

Read or say a nursery rhyme to the child. Repeat the rhyme. However, this time do not say the rhyming word. Have the child add the missing word. Ask him or her which words sounded alike and if he or she can think of any other words that sound like those words.

SMELLS GOOD!

Let kids' noses lead them through this initial-letter activity.

WHAT YOU'LL NEED: Variety of foods and other items with identifiable smells (as described below), scarf or blindfold

Children put their noses to work in this beginning-sound activity.

Collect several foods and other items with interesting smells, such as a slice of apple sprinkled with cinnamon, a lemon, an orange slice, a bar of soap, a bottle of perfume, toothpaste, a sprig of mint, a tea bag, an onion slice, and a banana.

Blindfold the child and let him or her smell an item and try to identify it. Then the child must say another word that begins with the same sound. For an added challenge, ask the child to write the letter that begins the name of the item.

RUN, WALK, JUMP, AND HOP

Hop for happiness and jump for joy in this beginning-sound activity.

Play an active game that focuses on the beginning sounds *H, R, W,* and *J.*

Say the word *hand* and ask the child to demonstrate hopping. Point out that the words *hand* and *hop* begin with the same sound. Tell the child that you will say words that begin like *hop* and also some that begin like *run, walk,* and *jump.* He or she should perform the activity (hop, run, walk, or jump) whose name has the same beginning sound as the word you say. Words to use might include *rope, wet, jar, head, win, jet, red,* and *hat.*

62

BIG BROWN BAG

Better be bright-eyed for this big bag of B's.

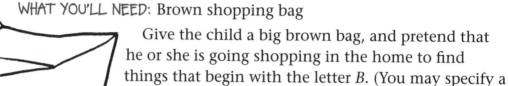

WHAT YOU'LL NEED: Brown shopping bag

Give the child a big brown bag, and pretend that he or she is going shopping in the home to find things that begin with the letter *B*. (You may specify a certain number of items if desired.) As the child finds an object, he or she should place it inside the bag. When the "shopping" is completed, ask him or her to tell you what was found and then discuss the objects, emphasizing the *B* sound. (Hints: ball, balloon, basket, bathrobe, bag.)

TASTE, TOUCH, SMELL

63

Learning the S sound can be "sweet," "soft," and "silky."

Play a sensory game that emphasizes the beginning sound *S*. First, help the child name the five senses: sight, sound, touch, taste, and smell.

Begin by asking a sense-related question that uses an *S* word. For example: "What can you find that feels *soft*?" Have the child find or name things in the house that answer the question. Then continue with other sense-related questions that contain *S* words, such as *silky, soapy, sour, sticky, sweet,* or *salty*.

64 WHAT IS MISSING?

Now you see it, now you don't. What could be missing?

WHAT YOU'LL NEED: Tray of items with different beginning sounds

Try this activity to enhance a child's visual awareness and beginning sound recognition.

On a tray, place a collection of various items, each beginning with a different letter (for example, boat, pencil, apple, cup, and sock). Begin with five items. Show the child the tray of items, and name them. Then ask the child to turn around so he or she cannot see the tray. Remove one of the items, and place it behind your back. Have the child turn around. Ask the child to identify the missing item. Give a clue by telling the child that the missing item begins with a certain letter (for example, *S*).

To make this activity more challenging, you can start with more objects; for younger children, you can start with as few as three objects. Reverse roles, and have the child remove an item from the tray. Ask him or her to give you a clue by telling you the beginning letter of the missing item.

RIDDLE TIME

How do you plant seeds in your garden?

Sow a row.

A B SEE

In this chapter, children get the "Alphabet Nitty Gritty" as they "Jump for *J*" and "Snap to It." These fun activities introduce children to printed letters. The skills practiced range from matching letter shapes to recognizing and naming specific letters. The chapter includes board games such as "Spider Man" and "ABC Concentration" as well as ideas to keep even the most active children interested as they walk down "Alphabet Avenue" or have fun "Bowling for Scholars."

65 · **EDIBLE LETTERS**

Start your day off right with a bowl of alphabet cereal.

WHAT YOU'LL NEED: Alphabet cereal

Letters are found in many places, and food is no exception.

Buy a box of alphabet cereal, and pour some in a dish. Ask the child to sort through the cereal to find the letters that make his or her name. The child can arrange these letters on the table. Say each letter as it is placed to emphasize letter awareness. After this activity, enjoy a bowl of cereal.

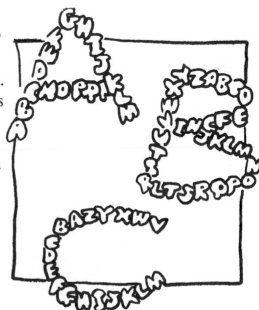

66 NAMES IN THE NEWS

Extra! Extra! Read all about it! Your name is in the news.

WHAT YOU'LL NEED: Old newspapers, blunt scissors, blank paper

Ask the child to search through an old newspaper to find one set of the letters that make up his or her first name. When the letters are found, have the child cut them out and arrange them to spell out the name on a blank piece of paper. Remember that the first letter needs to be a capital letter.

Variation: For an extra challenge, ask the child to find the letters of his or her middle and last names as well. This activity may be repeated by searching for and using different types, sizes, and colors of print.

CHECKING LICENSE PLATES 67

Search for license plate letters while you travel by car.

WHAT YOU'LL NEED: Paper, pencil

To pass the time when traveling in the car, give the child a sheet of paper with the alphabet printed on it in capital letters.

Have the child call out the letters that he or she sees on the license plates of other cars and then cross off those letters on the sheet of paper. Travel time will go by more quickly when the child is involved with this activity, and he or she will be exposed to reading mixed combinations of letters and numbers.

STEPPING STONES

68

Take these "steps" to learn letters and sounds.

WHAT YOU'LL NEED: 26 sheets of paper, markers

Let the child explore the many possibilities of this activity.

Write a capital *A* on one side of a sheet of paper and a lowercase *a* on the other side. Do the same for each letter of the alphabet. Spread the sheets of paper on the floor like stones, and see how the child uses these materials. He or she can arrange them in alphabetical order, or make a long path and say each letter as it is stepped on.

69

TELEPHONE DIRECTORY

Find names beginning with different letters using a recycled phone directory.

WHAT YOU'LL NEED: Old telephone directory, blunt scissors, envelope

Another source where many letters are found is a telephone directory.

Show the child an old telephone directory, and look through it together. Explain what is in a telephone directory. A good introduction to the directory is to look for and cut out the child's last name or a friend's name. Using blunt scissors, the child can also cut out names beginning with each letter of the alphabet. (You can use boldfaced names for easier cutting and viewing—or cut out groups of five or more consecutive names.) Have the child recognize that names always begin with a capital letter, that a telephone directory lists last names first, and that the book is arranged in alphabetical order. After the names are cut out and every letter has been found, place these cuttings in an envelope, saving them for the activity entitled "Telephone Directory II."

TELEPHONE DIRECTORY II

70

Forgot a telephone number? This directory can help.

WHAT YOU'LL NEED: Names cut out for "Telephone Directory" activity, sheet of paper, glue or clear tape

Have the child use the names in the envelope that were cut out for "Telephone Directory." The object now is for the child to organize these names in alphabetical order. (It may be easier for the child to spread all the names on the floor or table.)

When the names are arranged in alphabetical order, have the child begin with the *A* name, and glue or tape it onto the paper. Proceed through the alphabet. The names can be arranged as in a real telephone directory—in columns, proceeding from top to bottom and left to right.

71

WHAT IS THE LETTER?

Give a child a "feel" for the letters of the alphabet.

Another way for a child to experience letters is for you to "write" a letter on the child's back by slowly tracing it with your finger. Capital letters are probably the easiest to identify. Ask the child to guess the letter. He or she will have to concentrate on your motions and strokes to determine the correct letter. For an advanced child, spell out simple, three-letter words. Have the child guess the three letters and, if possible, determine the word.

WORD LETTER MATCH

72

Look for clues to solve this game, matching capital and lowercase letters.

WHAT YOU'LL NEED: Index cards, pen or marker

Knowledge of lowercase letters is necessary for reading printed materials. This activity helps the child recognize letters in lowercase form.

On index cards, write simple words, such as *cat, ball, fish, mat,* and *cake,* in capital letters. Write the same words on a second set of cards in lowercase letters. Have the child sound out the words and match the cards with the same word.

73

WORDS LIKE MY NAME

Help a child find words that begin with the same first letter as his or her name.

WHAT YOU'LL NEED: Old magazines, blunt scissors, sheet of paper, glue or clear tape

Have the child become aware of words that begin with the same letter as his or her first and/or last name.

Give the child blunt scissors and some old magazines (those with a lot of advertisements and big print will work best). Talk about the first letter in his or her name, and begin the search for words in the magazine beginning with that same letter. After the words are found and cut out, they may be pasted on paper. Read the words that were chosen aloud. Keep emphasizing that the words also have the same beginning sound as the child's name.

74 ...... LETTER SEARCH ......

Have fun looking at pictures to find special hidden letters.

WHAT YOU'LL NEED: Pictures from a magazine or travel brochure, pen or marker

This activity allows a child to look for hidden letters and then make a word out of them.

Take a picture from a magazine or travel brochure. Using a pen or marker, hide some letters in the photograph by blending all or parts of them into the lines, curves, and shapes of objects in the picture. Ideally, the letters must be written so that they are visible, yet thin enough so that the child's search will be somewhat challenging.

One way to start is to use the letters in the child's name. Try capital letters first and then lowercase letters. Give the child the picture and have him or her search for the letters in his or her name. When the letters are found, ask the child to say each one and show where it is.

NURSERY RHYME

- - - - - - - - - - -

Lucy Locket lost her pocket,
Kitty Fisher found it;
Not a penny in her purse
but a ribbon round it.

75 NEWSPAPER LETTERS

Use a newspaper to set up this letter-search activity.

WHAT YOU'LL NEED: Marker, newspaper page

This activity exposes the child to a newspaper, a medium in which letters and words are important.

Give the child a page from a newspaper, and ask him or her to search it for a particular letter. Every time that letter is found, have the child put a circle around it with a marker. You may limit this to capital or lowercase letters, or search for both. Try different letters, and have the child note the frequency of some letters (such as *E*) compared to others (for example, *X*).

FITTING LETTERS 76

*Matching capital and lowercase letters will be fun
with these puzzles.*

WHAT YOU'LL NEED: Index cards, marker or pen, blunt scissors

Using index cards positioned horizontally, you can make several (or all 26) letter cards. Write a capital letter on the left half of each card and the corresponding lowercase letter on the right half. Randomly cut the cards between the letters (using notches, angles, zig-zags, and curved cuts), then mix them up in a single pile.

The object of this activity is for the child to match the capital letter to its lowercase partner. The child will know that he or she made a correct match when the two halves fit together. You can begin this activity with only a few letters and eventually work to mixing and matching the entire alphabet.

SMALL, TALL, OR TAIL

77

Did you know that all lowercase letters can be grouped into one of three categories?

WHAT YOU'LL NEED: 26 alphabet cards, each showing one lowercase letter of the alphabet (and lined to show where the letter sits in relation to its baseline)

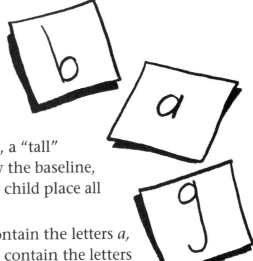

Categorizing lowercase letters will help the child learn and recall these letters.

Spread the lowercase alphabet cards on the floor or table. Pick out an example of a "small" letter (such as *a*), a "tall" letter (such as *b*), and a "tail" letter (one that goes below the baseline, such as *g*). Use these letters to start three piles. Have the child place all of the other letters into one of those three piles.

When the child is finished, the "small" pile should contain the letters *a, c, e, i, m, n, o, r, s, u, v, w, x,* and *z*. The "tall" pile should contain the letters *b, d, f, h, k, l,* and *t*. The "tail" pile should have the letters *g, j, p, q,* and *y*.

78

A CLOSER LOOK

Try this activity after you finish reading a story to a child.

WHAT YOU'LL NEED: Storybook

You can never read to a child too often. A child will develop a love of reading by your reading aloud to him or her. This also helps develop the child's vocabulary, letter recognition, letter sounds, intonation and inflections, and comprehension.

After reading a book to the child, ask him or her to point to a certain letter on the page and to identify it (for example, capital *T*, lowercase *w*).

79 ROLLING THE DIE

A simple roll of the die leads to learning letters—and words.

WHAT YOU'LL NEED: Cube-shaped wooden block or box, six pieces of paper small enough to be taped to the sides of the cube, clear tape, pen or marker

Find a cube-shaped wooden block or box. Choose any six letters of the alphabet, write them down on individual pieces of paper, and tape them to the cube (one letter on each side). Roll the cube as you would a die, then have the child call out the letter that appears on the top and say a word that begins with that letter. Change the letters periodically to reinforce the recognition of other letters and sounds.

PIZZA PUZZLE 80

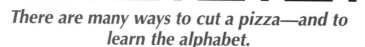

There are many ways to cut a pizza—and to learn the alphabet.

WHAT YOU'LL NEED: Pizza pan, construction paper cut in a circle to fit in the bottom of the pan, blunt scissors, marker or pen

Here's a puzzle to help children practice identifying letters.

Cut the paper circle into several pieces of varying shapes and sizes. Write a letter of the alphabet on each piece. Invite the child to put the puzzle together in the pan, naming the letter on each piece he or she uses. Begin with a puzzle that has only a few pieces, and work up to more complex puzzles.

81 — JUMP FOR J

Recognizing the letter J is fun when you get to jump for it.

WHAT YOU'LL NEED: At least 57 index cards (or cards made from poster board), marker

You can use letter cards for a variety of fun phonics activities.

Make one set of 26 alphabet cards in capital letters—one letter per card. Make another set of 26 cards using the lowercase letters—again, one letter per card. Make at least five extra cards for the letter *J*, some uppercase, some lowercase.

Show the letter *J* cards to the child, pointing out that in this activity the letter stands for the word *jump.* Shuffle the cards, and have the child crouch down as you show him or her the cards one by one. The child has to jump up each time you display a letter *J*. Encourage the child to call out every letter that he or she recognizes.

WHERE IS IT? — 82

How many objects can you find in your home starting with a particular letter of the alphabet?

WHAT YOU'LL NEED: Alphabet cards

An important step in learning to read is to be able to match a letter to its letter sound and to objects whose names have such sounds.

Hand the child an alphabet card (for example, the letter *D*). Ask him or her to look around the home for an object beginning with that letter (for example, a doll). Have the child say the letter and name the object to verify the match.

83 DON'T LOOK NOW

Pin the tail on the . . . alphabet?

WHAT YOU'LL NEED: Poster board or butcher paper, scarf to be used as a blindfold, marker, tape

Here's a twist on an old party favorite, "Pin the Tail on the Donkey." Use a marker to print the letters of the alphabet in random order on the poster board or butcher paper. Tape this letter chart to the back of a door.

Cover the child's eyes with the scarf, and turn him or her around two or three times. Tell the child to locate and put a finger on the chart. Take off the blindfold, and have the child identify the letter he or she is touching. Repeat until several different letters have been identified.

TONGUE TWISTER

Peter Piper picked a peck of pickled peppers;
A peck of pickled peppers Peter Piper picked;
If Peter Piper picked a peck of pickled peppers,
Where's the peck of pickled peppers Peter Piper picked?

MATCH ME

84

Try the magazine letter challenge. Locate lowercase letters to match capital letters.

WHAT YOU'LL NEED: Several children's magazines, alphabet cards (capital letters), blunt scissors

A subscription to a children's magazine can be very exciting for him or her. He or she may come to anticipate each issue and the opportunity to learn new things.

Save back issues of any children's magazines that you purchase or subscribe to. Ask the child to find a lowercase letter in the magazine that matches each capital letter on the alphabet cards, which you randomly present to him or her one card at a time. As each letter is found, the child cuts it out and places it on the letter card next to its corresponding capital.

85 # WOODEN ALPHABET BLOCKS

Build the entire alphabet using traditional wooden blocks.

WHAT YOU'LL NEED: Wooden alphabet blocks

Give the child a set of alphabet blocks, and ask him or her to arrange the blocks in alphabetical order. As the blocks are being arranged, have the child say each letter.

Variation: On the blocks that have pictures, the child can match the corresponding letter block to that picture block.

86 MENU SPECIALS

Waiting for your food to be served? This menu game helps time pass by quickly.

WHAT YOU'LL NEED: Menu

What can you do in a restaurant to involve a child until dinner is served? Keep your menu, and play this game.

Ask the waiter or waitress if you may keep the menu until dinner is served. Give the child the menu, and have him or her locate a menu item beginning with a certain letter. You can be specific and state that it must be a capital or lowercase letter. When the child finds a word beginning with that letter, have him or her point to it and say the letter. Ask the child to look at all the letters in the word and, by sounding out the letters, try to determine what the menu item is.

NURSERY RHYME

Once I saw a little robin
go hop, hop, hop;
I asked the little robin
to stop, stop, stop.

He blinked his eye and turned around
with a peep, peep, peep,
and across the yard he went
with a leap, leap, leap.

87

LETTER ORDER

CBA or ABC? When kids know their letters, they can put them in order.

WHAT YOU'LL NEED: Set of letter cards with capital letters, set of letter cards with lowercase letters

Children can manipulate letter cards to learn alphabetical order.

Remove the capital letter cards *A* through *F* from the first set of cards. Mix the six cards. Ask the child to lay the cards out in alphabetical order. When he or she is ready for more challenging activities, use additional capital letters and then lowercase letters.

ALPHABET AVENUE

88

Kids can walk the walk and talk the talk on this educational street.

WHAT YOU'LL NEED: Butcher paper, marker

On a large sheet of butcher paper, print two or three large letters with a marker. Make each letter approximately two feet high. You might start with the vowels *A, E, I, O,* and *U* or with the consonants *B, D, P, S,* and *T.* Put the sheet on the floor and ask the child to walk on or around each letter while saying its name. After the child has mastered these letters, make a new sheet with new letters.

89 ALPHABET STAMPS

It's as easy as 1, 2, 3: All you have to do is dip, press, and print.

WHAT YOU'LL NEED: Alphabet stamps, stamp pad, paper

In this activity, the child uses small muscles in the hand to hold a letter stamp and print letters while learning letter recognition.

Get a stamp pad. Have the child take an alphabet letter stamp, press it onto the pad, and stamp the letter onto the paper to make a print of the letter. As each letter is printed, ask the child what letter it is. Discuss the lines of the letter. Are they curved or straight, or does the letter have both?

Continue printing letters. Ask the child to try to spell his or her name or other simple words. Have the child read what he or she has printed.

NOW I KNOW MY ABCs 90

Singing the "Alphabet Song" can be a visual as well as a musical experience.

WHAT YOU'LL NEED: Letter cards for the alphabet, recording of the "Alphabet Song" (optional)

Use music to make learning the alphabet fun. Sing the "Alphabet Song" with the child until he or she is familiar with it. You might also play one of the many recordings of the song. Place the stack of letter cards face down on the table, but in alphabetical order. Sing the alphabet song slowly. Have the child pick up and show each letter card as you sing its name in the song.

91 ALPHABET NITTY GRITTY

Who says reading is rough? Only when fingers do the walking.

WHAT YOU'LL NEED: Sandpaper, blunt scissors

Some children learn better through activities that concentrate on touch. Cut letter shapes out of sandpaper. Invite the child to trace each letter with his or her finger while saying which letter it is.

FISHING FOR LETTERS 92

Bait that hook and cast your line. See what fish letters can be caught.

WHAT YOU'LL NEED: Dowel rod, string, construction paper, blunt scissors, marker or pen, magnet, paper clips

Here is an opportunity for a child to go fishing—for letters.

Using several sheets of construction paper, cut out 26 fish shapes. Write one letter of the alphabet on both sides of each fish. Affix a paper clip to each fish. To make the fishing pole, take a dowel rod and tie a piece of string onto one end. At the end of the string, tie a magnet. To set the atmosphere for this activity, place the paper fish in a bathtub, dish pan, or inflatable swimming pool. (They should not contain water.)

The task for the child is to use the fishing pole to catch a fish. The magnet will attract the paper clip on each fish. When a fish is caught, have the child pull it gently off the magnet and say the letter.

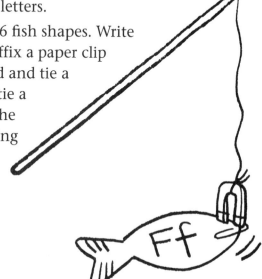

BOWLING FOR SCHOLARS

93

Children who know their letters can bowl a perfect game.

WHAT YOU'LL NEED: Ten empty plastic soft-drink bottles, masking tape or self-stick labels, marker, large beach ball or plastic ball

This activity combines bowling and letter identification.

Put a strip of masking tape or a label on each bottle, and print a different letter on each one. Set the bottles up in a row and have the child roll the ball toward the "pins."

Ask the child to identify the letter on each pin he or she knocks down. If the child identifies the letter correctly, the pin stays knocked down. If the child cannot identify the letter, the pin is set back up. Continue playing until all pins have been knocked down and all letters correctly identified.

94

LETTER PATTERNS

Children can match letters even if they can't identify them.

WHAT YOU'LL NEED: Two sets of letter cards

Even before children can identify letters by name, they can recognize their shapes.

You'll need two matching sets of letter cards. Randomly select three letter cards from one set, and place them in a row on a table. Give the child the other set of cards, and ask him or her to find the matching letter cards and lay them down in the same order. Increase the difficulty by making a series of more letters.

95 ALPHABET PHOTO ALBUM

Neighborhood adventurers and photography enthusiasts will find this activity eye-opening.

WHAT YOU'LL NEED: Camera, scrapbook or photo album

This is an exciting outdoor activity that helps children learn the alphabet—as well as operate a camera.

Get a camera (a disposable one will do), and go on a walk through the neighborhood or a nearby town or city with the child. Ask him or her to look for each letter of the alphabet on as many different street signs and store signs as possible. Take one picture of each letter found. You might want to show the child how to use the camera so he or she can help.

Don't try to get the whole alphabet in one outing. Develop the pictures, and help the child put them in a scrapbook or album in alphabetical order. Enjoy one or two more outings in which you look for the specific letters you're missing to complete the set.

96 STAR TREK

There's a whole universe of fun in this alphabet board game.

WHAT YOU'LL NEED: Construction paper, poster board, marker or pen, blunt scissors, glue or clear tape, die and markers from a board game

Invite the child to play a letter identification game with an outer-space theme.

To prepare the game board, cut 15 to 26 star shapes and one moon shape from the construction paper. Paste or tape the stars in an S-shaped path on the poster board, with the moon at the end. Write letters in random order on the stars.

To play the game, take turns throwing the die and moving markers along the star path. In order to continue along the path, the player must name the letter on each star he or she lands on. If the player does not name the letter correctly, he or she must go back to the beginning of the path. Continue until one player reaches the moon.

BIG LETTER, LITTLE LETTER 97

Confusion over capitals? Create a color code.

WHAT YOU'LL NEED: Paper, marker or pen, crayons

Help children practice recognizing the capital and lowercase forms of letters.

Draw a circle and divide it into six equal parts. In the top three parts, write the capital letters *A, B,* and *C.* In the bottom three parts, write the lowercase letters *b, a,* and *c.* Ask the child to find each matching capital and lowercase letter and shade the two parts with the same color.

SPIDER MAN

Fans of creepy crawling creatures will enjoy making fuzzy spiders.

WHAT YOU'LL NEED: Cotton balls, 18″ to 24″ length of yarn, construction paper, glue, clear tape, blunt scissors, pen, poster board or butcher paper

Invite children to play a board game that uses their ability to recognize like and different letters.

First, make a spider game piece for each player. Use a cotton ball for each spider's body. Tape eight short pieces of yarn to the bottom of the cotton ball for legs. Glue two construction-paper eyes on the top of the cotton ball. For the game board, draw a path of squares on the poster board or a sheet of butcher paper. At the end of the path, draw a spider web. In each square, write a pair of letters, sometimes the same *(B, B)* and sometimes different *(E, F)*. Players take turns moving a spider to each square on the path and telling whether the letters on the square are the same or different.

LETTER LADDER

The sky's the limit in this letter-identification game.

WHAT YOU'LL NEED: Poster board or butcher paper, letter cards, marker or pen

Use a ladder to show a child's progress in letter identification.

Draw a ladder with six or seven rungs. (Make the space between each two rungs large enough to display a letter card.) Place a letter card on each rung. Challenge the child to move up the ladder by identifying the letter on each rung.

SAY A WORD

Spin the arrow and learn to say a new word.

WHAT YOU'LL NEED: Lightweight cardboard, brad fastener, marker or pen, compass, blunt scissors

Use a compass to draw a circle 8″ in diameter on a piece of cardboard. Then draw lines to divide the circle into six equal sections. At the center point of the circle, make a small hole with the scissors. Cut out a simple arrow about 3″ long and 1″ wide from another piece of cardboard to use as the spinner. Put a brad fastener through the middle of the arrow and the center of the wheel.

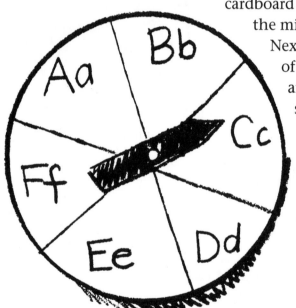

Next, write a single letter in each of the six sections of the circle. The child spins the arrow on the wheel and says a word that begins with the letter in the section where the arrow comes to rest.

Variation: To make this activity more challenging, increase the number of sections. For the child who can read, in addition to saying a word beginning with a particular letter, the child should also spell the word.

RIDDLE TIME

How do you ask for tiny green vegetables?
(Pass the peas, please.)

101 ALL ABOARD!

Kids are conductors and animals are commuters in this transportation game.

WHAT YOU'LL NEED: Toy animals, letter cards, several shoe boxes or similar containers

Use children's love of imaginative play to help them learn letter identification.

Help the child create a train out of shoe boxes or some other convenient containers. Have him or her line up the toy animals and place a letter card by each one. Explain that the cards are the animals' tickets. In order to board the "passengers," the child must be the conductor and identify the letter on each animal's card.

LETTER TIC-TAC-TOE 102

This game helps kids learn letters—up, down, and sideways.

WHAT YOU'LL NEED: Three sheets of construction paper (including one red sheet and one yellow sheet), marker or pen, blunt scissors

Play tic-tac-toe with a phonics twist. Make a tic-tac-toe board on a sheet of construction paper. Write a different letter on each of the nine squares of the board. Next, cut two sets of square markers, five red ones and five yellow ones, that fit in the tic-tac-toe squares. Give each player one set of markers.

The first player chooses a square. In order to put a marker there, he or she names the letter in the square. The game continues until one player covers a row across, down, or diagonally or until the board is filled.

103 PICK A NUMBER

All numbers are lucky when kids use them to learn letters.

WHAT YOU'LL NEED: Paper, 10 cards with numbers 1 through 10, pen or pencil

This activity helps children recognize both letters and numbers.

On a sheet of paper, write the numbers 1 through 10 in a column, and write a letter by each number. Shuffle the number cards and place them in a stack. Instruct the child to take the top card, match it to a number on the sheet, and name the corresponding letter.

If the child identifies the letter correctly, he or she keeps the number card. If the child is incorrect, the card is placed at the bottom of the stack. When all the letters have been identified correctly, make a list with different letters.

CARD CLAP 104

Match a pair of letters and put your hands together.

WHAT YOU'LL NEED: Two matching sets of letter cards

Use letter cards for this letter-recognition game. Begin by using only the *A* through *M* cards of both sets. Shuffle each set of cards. Place the two sets in side-by-side piles.

Pick up and display the top card of each set. Tell the child to clap if the two cards show the same letter, in which case you put the matching cards aside. If the two cards do not match, place each one at the bottom of its pile. Continue until all matching pairs have been identified. Then put the cards back into their sets, shuffle each set, and repeat the activity. Add new matching pairs of cards to the sets when the child has mastered the first half of the alphabet.

WHERE WAS IT?

Test your memory and find the matching letter.

WHAT YOU'LL NEED: 16 paper cards (2″ × 2″ each), a pen or marker

Use this activity to enhance a child's visual memory.

Make a set of two alphabet cards for each of any eight letters. Depending on the child's developmental level, the matching cards may both be capital letters (*A* and *A*) or lowercase letters (*a* and *a*), or else a combination of the two (*A* and *a*).

Shuffle the 16 cards (eight pairs of letters) and arrange them face down in a square (four rows of four). Ask the child to turn over any two cards. If they match, he or she can keep that set and take another turn. If they do not match, the cards must be put back in the same place, face down. It is then the next player's turn (yours or a second child's). To be successful in this game, a child will have to remember where at least some of the revealed but unmatched cards are. The game ends when all of the cards are matched. Who has the most cards?

106 LETTER SCULPTURE

Mold youngsters' minds with three-dimensional letters.

WHAT YOU'LL NEED: Shoe box, sand, plaster of paris, water

Making three-dimensional letters enables a child to experience the alphabet in a new way.

Put some moist sand in a shoe box. Help the child write letters in the sand. Let the child choose the letters to write, such as the initials of his or her first and last name. Make the letter shapes in the sand deep and wide. Mix the plaster of paris according to the directions on the package, and pour it into the letter shapes. Let the letters dry. Take the letters out of the box and display your three-dimensional letters.

SEEK AND SAY 107

Find a toy and match it with the right letter card.

WHAT YOU'LL NEED: Objects to hide, letter cards

Children love finding hidden objects. In this game, they will find objects and identify the beginning sounds of the objects' names.

Lay the letter cards out in rows. Hide objects, such as a variety of toys (ball, doll, teddy bear, car, top, jack-in-the-box, bat), around the room or yard. Have the child search for the toys. After finding a toy, he or she must locate the letter card that stands for the beginning sound in the toy's name in order to keep the card. Continue until all the objects are found and the beginning sounds of their names are identified. This is a good game for a group of children.

108 C IS FOR COLOR

The only thing more fun than matching letters is making lots of noise when you're finished!

WHAT YOU'LL NEED: Crayons, two sheets of wax paper, two sheets of regular paper, small pencil sharpener, iron

Here's a creative, colorful way to learn the letter *C*.

Use new or old crayons. Tear off two sheets of wax paper measuring approximately 8½″ × 11″. Draw a large letter *C* on a sheet of paper, and tell the child that it stands for the beginning sound in the word *color*.

Have the child sharpen several crayons in a portable pencil sharpener, forming the shavings into the shape of a large *C* on one sheet of wax paper. When the letter is finished, put the other sheet of wax paper on top to cover it.

Next, put another sheet of paper on top of the wax paper, and press the top sheet briefly with a warm iron. The shavings will melt to form a multicolored letter. Have the child display the picture and think of other words that begin with the *C* sound.

PHONICS FUN FACT

The English alphabet is one of about 50 alphabets in the modern world. Although these alphabets may differ in the number and design of their letters, they all are based on the idea of using symbols to represent the sounds of language.

109 TACTILE ALPHABET

Make an alphabet book containing textured letters.

WHAT YOU'LL NEED: 26 sheets of construction paper, glue, marker, textured materials found around the house (see below), O-rings, hole puncher

There are some things that children can learn just by using their sense of touch. In this activity, the child will make a "tactile" alphabet book.

For each letter of the alphabet, write the capital and its matching lowercase letter on a sheet of construction paper. Make the letters reasonably large. Outline the letters in glue—spread wide is best. Help the child place any textured material that begins with the same letter (such as glitter for *G* or peanut shells for *P*) on the glue-outlined letters. Do one letter at a time so the glue will not dry before you can finish.

Additional suggestions for textured materials you can use for specific letters (feel free to use substitutes) are:

- apple seeds for the letter *A*
- buttons for the letter *B*
- cotton for *C*
- dots (left over from paper puncher) for *D*
- eggshells for *E*
- feathers for *F*
- granola for *G*
- hay for *H*
- ink for *I*
- "jewels" from old costume jewelry for *J*
- old keys for *K*
- lace for *L*

- magnetic strips for *M*
- nutshells for *N*
- oatmeal for *O*
- peanuts for *P*
- bendable Q-tips for *Q*
- rubber bands for *R*
- sand for *S*
- tape for *T*
- uncooked noodles for *U*
- velvet for *V*

- wallpaper for *W*
- alphabet cereal X's for *X*
- yarn for *Y*
- zippers for *Z*

When all 26 textured letters are made, punch holes on the left sides of each sheet of paper and connect the pages with O-rings. When the book is completed, ask the child to trace and feel the letters, name the letters, and then tell you what was used to make the letters. Help the child design a cover for the book.

SALT AND PEPPER

Kids who practice this game can become seasoned players.

WHAT YOU'LL NEED: Construction paper (various colors, but including one sheet each of white, red, and black), white crayon, black crayon

Children can learn letters by associating them with everyday items.

Make a deck of 20 construction-paper cards that has 10 cards of various colors, plus five white cards and five black cards. Have both players use sheets of red paper to make scorecards, writing *S* in white crayon and *P* in black crayon at the top of the page.

Shuffle the 20 cards, and then take turns choosing one. Each player should write an *S* in the *S* (for *salt*) column in white when a white card is chosen, or the letter *P* in the *P* (for *pepper*) column in black when a black card is chosen. Continue until one player has written five of either letter, going through the cards again if necessary.

TWO OF A KIND

Have you noticed that the letter B looks like two bumps on a stick?

WHAT YOU'LL NEED: Paper, pen

Here's a simple activity that helps children practice seeing likenesses and differences between letters but does not require letter identification.

Write a row of letters on a sheet of paper. For example: *C, E, C, D*. Point to each letter and ask the child to describe it. When you point to the letter *C*, the child might say, "It looks like a circle with an opening." Then have the child point to the two letters that are alike.

LETTERS ON-LINE

It's never too early to join the computer age. Kids can do just that while they learn letters in this simple activity.

WHAT YOU'LL NEED: Computer

This activity can be done at home or school, if there's a computer available. Otherwise, try the library. Even the library's on-line catalog computer would work for this exercise.

Have the child type any letter on the keyboard. When it appears on the screen, ask the child to name it. If possible, use larger type and decorative fonts to keep the child's interest. For a more advanced child, you name the letter and ask the child to find it on the keyboard and type it in.

KNOCK-KNOCK JOKE

Knock, knock

Who's there?

C

C who?

C what you can do.

113 ⬤ LETTER RATTLES

The only thing more fun than matching letters is making lots of noise when you're finished!

WHAT YOU'LL NEED: Masking tape or adhesive labels, marker or pen, five or six empty coffee cans with plastic lids, set of alphabet blocks

Children will compare uppercase and lowercase versions of letters in this activity.

Choose any five letters of the alphabet. Write the capital letter version on one piece of masking tape (or label) and the matching lowercase letter form on another. Put the capital letters on the empty cans and the lowercase letters on the detached lids, which should be placed nearby.

Lay out the blocks. Ask the child to find the blocks with the letters indicated on each of the cans, then put them inside the containers. Next, have the child find the lids with the matching lowercase letters and put them on the appropriate cans.

Note that cans with blocks in them can be used as rhythm instruments.

RIDDLE TIME

How does an elephant take a shower? (with its nose hose)

What is another name for a sweet rabbit? (a honey bunny)

What do you call dog spaghetti? (noodles for poodles)

ALPHABET HUNT

Using a clipboard will add to kids' fun as they conduct this official alphabet search.

WHAT YOU'LL NEED: Letter cards, legal pad or clipboard, marker or pen

Here's a great way to brush up on all of the letters in the alphabet.

Remove any one letter card from a complete set of letter cards representing the entire alphabet. Place the remaining 25 cards around a room in plain sight, but in random order, then help the child write the letters of the alphabet in proper order down the page on a legal pad.

Instruct the child to go around the room and put a check mark on the pad beside the appropriate letter as he or she finds each card. When the child has finished this task, ask him or her to identify the letter on the pad that does not have a check mark. For beginners, use only the first 10 letters of the alphabet.

MUSICAL ALPHABET

Here's a letter-recognition game that will be music to kids' ears.

WHAT YOU'LL NEED: 26 index cards, marker or pen, radio (or cassette or CD player)

The child's listening skills will get a workout in this activity.

Make a letter card for each letter of the alphabet. Lay the cards in a big circle on the floor, spaced about one child's step apart.

Tell the child to walk around the outside of the circle, one step per letter, when the music starts playing. When the music stops, the child must stop and name a word that begins with the sound represented by the letter he or she is standing next to. Repeat until many different letters have been used.

116 SNAP TO IT

Use clothespins to avoid "hang-ups" when practicing the alphabet.

WHAT YOU'LL NEED: Large cardboard box, alphabet cards, plastic clothespins

In this activity, children find and display the letters of the alphabet.

Place the alphabet cards in a stack or spread them out on a table. Put the box on the floor or on a table with the open side up. Name a letter. Have the child find the card with the letter you named and attach it to the edge of the box with a clothespin. Continue with other letters.

You might use the entire alphabet or choose only a few cards, depending on the child's skill level. As a variation, make one set of cards with only capital letters and another with only lowercase letters. Have the child find and match the letter pairs and clip them together on the edge of the box.

ALPHABET BRACELET 117

Children will find this initial-letter search charming.

WHAT YOU'LL NEED: Construction paper, blunt scissors, masking tape, household objects

Here's an opportunity for children to wear the alphabet on their wrists.

Cut out the letters *A* through *F,* approximately 1½″ high, from various colors of construction paper. (Older children may use blunt scissors to cut letters drawn by adults.) Put masking tape loosely around the child's wrist with the sticky side out. Choose one of the construction-paper letters. Have the child find an object in the house that begins with that letter. When the object is found, the letter may be put on the bracelet. Continue until all of the letters are on the bracelet.

Variations: Search for objects outside, or use a different group of letters.

MEMORIES

▼▼▼▼▼▼▼▼▼▼▼▼▼▼▼▼▼▼▼▼▼▼▼▼▼▼▼▼▼

Make a keepsake album of a special field trip.

WHAT YOU'LL NEED: Camera, photographs, paper, glue or clear tape, pen, hole puncher, string

A field trip can be a rewarding experience for a child. In this activity, a lesson on language can be incorporated into the experience.

Select a special place to visit with the child—for example, a zoo, a farm, or a circus. While on this trip, have the child take photographs. (Your assistance may be needed with the camera.) After the film has been developed, the child can paste or tape the photos on paper. Allow space for captions.

Have the child dictate a sentence to describe what happened in each photo. Write this description below each photo so the child sees the process of sounding out letters and putting them in written (printed) form. Punch holes in each page and, using string, tie the pages together to form a book. Save a special photo for the cover, then decide on a title for the book and write it on the cover. The child now has a special book about a special trip.

119 · · · · · · · · · · · · · · · · · · CATS AND DOGS · · · · · · · · · · · · · ·

Follow a four-legged friend in this simple board game.

WHAT YOU'LL NEED: Pictures of a cat and a dog, poster board, die and markers from board game, marker or pen

Here's a board game that teaches children the letters *C* and *D*.

Make a board game with two paths of 12 squares each. Put a picture of a cat at the end of one path and a picture of a dog at the end of the other. Write the letter *C* in several squares of the path to the cat and other letters in the rest of the squares. Write the letter *D* in several squares of the path to the dog, using other letters in the rest of the squares.

Two players take turns rolling a die and moving markers along their paths. If a player on the cat path lands on a *C*, he or she continues. If not, the player loses a turn. The player on the dog path continues only if he or she lands on a *D*. Play until one player reaches the end of a path.

PHONICS FUN FACT
- -

Fifteen capital letters are called stick letters and are made with horizontal, vertical, or diagonal lines—*A, E, F, H, I, K, L, M, N, T, V, W, Y, X,* and *Z.* Circle letters include *O, Q,* and *C.*

SCRAMBLED LETTERS

120

Even kids who don't like eggs will have fun with this "egg-citing" activity.

WHAT YOU'LL NEED: Construction paper, blunt scissors, three egg cartons, marker

Sorting letters into egg cartons is one way to recognize letter likenesses and differences.

Cut off the tops of the egg cartons so that you have three bottoms with 12 hollow sections each. With a marker, print a letter on the bottom of each section, with *A* to *I* in the first carton, *J* to *R* in the second carton, and *S* to *Z* in the third carton. Using construction paper, cut out 26 circles approximately one inch in diameter and print one letter of the alphabet on each one. Put the letter discs in a small container and mix them. Have the child take the discs out one at a time and put each into its matching egg-carton section.

121

RED LETTER DAY

Teach a child the alphabet in less than one month.

WHAT YOU'LL NEED: Red pen or pencil, paper

Devoting a day to one letter helps focus a child's learning.

At the beginning of the day, assign a letter to look for. Write the letter in red, and display it in the kitchen. Ask the child to look for it in the home—on cans and boxes in the kitchen, in magazines and newspapers, on television. Each time the child finds the letter, he or she writes it in red on a sheet of paper.

NATURAL LETTERS

122

Your environment is a source for many letter shapes.
How many can you find?

Many letters of the alphabet can be seen if one looks closely at different objects.

Inside the house, is the letter *H* visible if you look at the legs of a chair? Do you see a *Y* when looking at the branches of a plant? Outdoors, can you see an *L* by looking at the side of the steps? Can you see an *A* in the frame of your swing set? See how many letters you can find in your environment.

123 # ALPHABET ACTIVITY BOOK

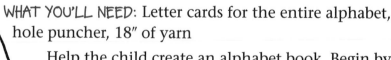

*C **is for** creating. **Make an alphabet book filled with activity ideas.***

WHAT YOU'LL NEED: Letter cards for the entire alphabet, hole puncher, 18" of yarn

Help the child create an alphabet book. Begin by punching one or two holes in each letter card and using the yarn to tie the cards together in order. Go through the letter book and have the child suggest an activity for each letter; for example, *A* (*ask* a question), *B* (*bat* a ball), *C* (*cook* a meal), *D* (*dig* a hole). Suggest that the child draw and color a picture to illustrate each activity. Later, the child can choose a page and perform the activity.

124 RED LIGHT, GREEN LIGHT

Follow the traffic signals on the road to higher learning.

WHAT YOU'LL NEED: Set of letter cards, red and green construction paper, blunt scissors, glue

This simple game utilizes children's understanding of traffic signals.

Cut red and green dots out of construction paper and glue them at the top of each letter card. Make about a third of the dots red and the rest green. Shuffle the cards. Have the child go through the cards one at a time and identify the letter on each card that has a green "light" (dot). When the child comes to a card with a red "light," his or her turn is over. Players can continue taking turns in this manner.

Variation: Play the game with letter cards made of red and green circles cut from construction paper.

CITY SEARCH 125

Where can you visit today? Search the map for a clue.

WHAT YOU'LL NEED: State map, marker or pen

Write the letters of the alphabet at the top of a large map of your state of residence. Locate the town or city where you live and place an *X* there. Have the child search for cities or towns that begin with different letters of the alphabet, and circle those locations when he or she finds them. At the top of the map, where the alphabet is written, cross off letters that represent towns or cities that have been located.

Toledo
Cleveland
Dayton
Columbus
Cincinnati

126 LETTERS IN THE MAIL

Open your own post office to reinforce letter recognition.

WHAT YOU'LL NEED: Letter cards, six blank envelopes, six shoe boxes, drawing paper, crayon or marker

Children can learn letters and increase their dexterity by creating their own "mail."

Hold up a letter card. Have the child use a crayon or marker to write the letter on an envelope and on the side of one of the shoe boxes. Ask the child to draw a picture of an object whose name begins with the letter on the envelope. Show the child how to fold the drawing, put it into the envelope, and seal the envelope (or put the flap inside the envelope).

Follow the same procedure until you have six different drawings in six envelopes, each one representing a different letter, and six shoe boxes, each one with a matching letter on its side. Shuffle the six "letters" and have the child "mail" each one in the appropriate shoe box. The next day, the child can receive his or her mail, further reinforcing letter recognition skills.

TONGUE TWISTERS

Lazy Lucy Lion licked a lemon lollipop.
Billy Bear bought a big balloon for baby Bobby.

127 ABC FLIPS

Flip the letter card. This activity is self-correcting.

WHAT YOU'LL NEED: Index cards, marker, lowercase alphabet cards

Capital letters are the first set of letters that a child learns. Next come the lowercase letters. Capital letters serve as the point of reference in this activity, which is intended to help the child learn lowercase letters.

To make a flip card, take a 3″ × 5″ index card and fold it in half so the card stands up. On the exposed surface, write a capital letter. Write the matching lowercase letter on the half covered by the capital letter flap.

Stand up the flip cards so the child can see all of the capital letters. Give the child the lowercase alphabet cards one letter at a time, and have him or her place each card by the matching capital letter on the flip card. The child can lift the flap to see if the lowercase letter matches the one that he or she selected.

ABC CONCENTRATION **128**

Alike or different? Let kids decide in this game.

WHAT YOU'LL NEED: Ten letter cards

Recognizing whether two letters are alike or different is an important reading skill. Shuffle 10 letter cards (five pairs of matching letters), and lay them out face up in two rows. Invite the child to put the five pairs of matching letters together.

Variation: Make one set of matching letters uppercase, the other set lowercase. You can also increase the number of cards used.

EYE TO HAND

Children need to develop both small-muscle coordination and eye-hand coordination as they learn to read and write. Chapter 3 activities provide fun ways to do both. Manipulating small objects, as in "Macaroni Letters," is a great way to help children improve small-muscle coordination. In other activities, children put together snake puzzles, pretend to read books, and twist pipe cleaners into letters—all important ways to work on eye-hand coordination.

129 REPTILE FAMILY

Even squeamish kids will like these colorful snake puzzles.

WHAT YOU'LL NEED: Construction paper, pen or marker, blunt scissors, plastic container

Here's a personalized puzzle that helps children recognize several kinds of likenesses and differences.

Make several snakes by drawing and cutting out squiggly snake shapes from different colors of construction paper. Along each snake, write the name of a family member or friend in large letters with space between the letters. Cut each snake into pieces with a letter on each piece. Put all the pieces into a container and mix them. Have the child put each snake back together by matching colors, letters, and edges.

130 WALKING THE TIGHTROPE

▼▼▼▼▼▼▼▼▼▼▼▼▼▼▼▼▼▼▼▼▼▼▼▼▼▼▼▼▼▼

Keeping one's balance is necessary to walk the letter tightrope. Be careful.

WHAT YOU'LL NEED: Rope cut in lengths of 4'

The challenge of walking a tightrope is exciting to a child. The motor skills necessary for balancing have to be used in this activity.

Take a piece (or pieces) of rope, and outline a very large letter (capital or lowercase) on the floor. The goal of this activity is for the child to "tightrope-walk" this letter. Make sure that, as the child is walking this letter, he or she is moving in the way that the letter is properly formed (top to bottom and left to right). Also, arms can be extended sideways to simulate the moves of a tightrope walker.

Variation: For an additional challenge, the child can walk sideways, moving on one foot next to the other; or, the child can be asked to cross one foot over the other.

STRING LETTERS 131

String 'em up! Use common string to form letters.

WHAT YOU'LL NEED: Pieces of string, paper and pen (optional)

Manipulating string requires the child to use muscles necessary for fine motor coordination.

Using different thicknesses and lengths of string, a child can form letters of the alphabet. For example, the string can be swirled into the letter *S*, or it can be zig-zagged to form a *Z*. Try to describe each letter the child makes using a word that begins with that letter. For example, point out the swirling *S*, the zig-zagged *Z*, and the curved *C*. For younger children, it may be helpful to begin with sheets of paper that have letters drawn on them already.

ABC STRIPS

132

Children who master this game won't be puzzled about alphabetical order.

WHAT YOU'LL NEED: Construction paper, marker or pen, blunt scissors

This activity helps children practice putting letters in alphabetical order.

Draw lines on a sheet of construction paper to divide it into four horizontal strips. Have the child write the letters *A, B, C,* and *D*—one on each strip. Cut the strips apart, and shuffle them. Then ask the child to put the strips back together in the correct order. Make other puzzles using other sets of four letters in alphabetical order.

133

DIGIT LETTERS

What letters can you make with your fingers?

Making letters with your fingers can be fun, yet challenging. It can also help a child who is having difficulty distinguishing between similar letters—lowercase *b* and *d,* for example.

With your left hand, use the middle finger, pointer finger, and thumb to form what will look like the signal for "okay": The pointer finger and thumb form a circle, with the rest of the fingers lining up straight in a single row. When you have done that, a lowercase *b* has been made. Do the same finger formations with your right hand to make a lowercase *d.*

If you place these two letter formations side by side, they kind of look like a bed with two pillows. Seeing this, the child can then associate the beginning sound *b* and the ending sound of *d* in the word *bed.* This helps him or her remember the differences between the two letters, and it reinforces the process of reading from left to right. See how many other finger letters the child can make.

PICTURE THIS

134

*Look carefully at a picture and you'll see all
kinds of things.*

WHAT YOU'LL NEED: Detailed "action" picture

As a child learns to read, interpreting pictures
becomes a big part of the language process.

In this activity, the child is asked to look
very closely at a detailed action picture
and describe what he or she sees. A child
who cannot read will name specific
objects that are seen—for example, a ball,
a girl, a flower. A beginning reader is often
able to describe what he or she sees with
greater detail. As the child is telling you what object
he or she sees, ask him or her what the beginning letter is.
Then write the word down for the child to see.

135

CHANGE IT!

Sneaky things can happen in this alphabet memory game.

WHAT YOU'LL NEED: Set of letter cards

Memory games can help children develop the visualization skills essential to reading.

Shuffle the cards and lay down three cards in a row face-up. Have the child study the
cards so that he or she will remember them. Ask the child to turn around, then add one
card or take one away. Ask him or her to turn back around and tell you what has changed.
As the child becomes more adept at the game, make more complex changes, such as
replacing one card with another.

136   READ TO ME

For a change of pace, ask a child to read you a story.

WHAT YOU'LL NEED: Children's picture books

Pretending to read helps children prepare to do the real thing.

Ask the child to read you a book. Read the title together. Then show the child how to turn the pages from the beginning to the end of the book. Encourage the child to tell you the story in the book by looking at the pictures. Ask him or her to find two words that look alike. Say the two words to the child, pointing out letters that are the same.

 FINGERPRINT LETTERS   137

Paint with your fingers, and discover the curves and lines in letters.

WHAT YOU'LL NEED: Tempera paint, white construction paper, clean Styrofoam meat tray

In this activity, the child uses paint and his or her finger to create letters.

Place some tempera paint on a clean Styrofoam meat tray. Have the child select one of his or her fingers (the pointer finger is probably best) and lay it down lengthwise on the paint. Ask the child to press the painted finger against the construction paper, making a fingerprint.

Next, help the child form a letter of the alphabet out of a series of fingerprints. Let him or her dip the selected finger back into the paint as needed. When the letter is dry, examine it together. Point out the different types of curved lines that appear in fingerprints.

ABC STAR

Follow the letter dots and see what shines.

WHAT YOU'LL NEED: Follow-the-dot picture, pencil, tissue paper, regular paper

To help a child learn the sequence of the alphabet, ask him or her to connect a series of dots to form a picture.

The child will have to draw a line from letters *A* to *B*, *B* to *C*, and so on until an object appears. As the child masters the alphabet, the pictures can be made more complex.

Start by drawing (or tracing) a simple, easily recognizable object on a sheet of tissue paper. Transfer this image by placing the tissue paper on top of a regular sheet of paper and pressing dots along the object's outline at regular intervals. Mark these dots on the paper with a sequence of letters beginning with *A*, and have the child connect the dots by following the sequence of the alphabet.

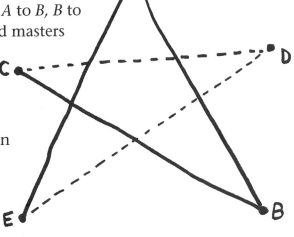

PHONICS FUN FACT

No other language has more words spelled the same way, but pronounced differently than English. Consider: *heard—beard, low—how, paid—said, break—speak, five—give, four—tour,* and *ache—mustache.*

TOM TURKEY

Kids don't have to wait till Thanksgiving to make and display this fine feathered friend.

WHAT YOU'LL NEED: Pencil, different-colored sheets of construction paper, blunt scissors, glue, clear tape, paper plate, pipe cleaners

Teach a child to make a turkey—and master the letter *T*.

First, ask the child to identify the beginning sound in the words *Tom Turkey* and then name other words with the same beginning sound. Next, draw a pattern for a feather on a sheet of construction paper, and cut it out with blunt scissors. Have the child trace the pattern onto several different-colored sheets of construction paper, cutting them out as you did. Help the child glue or tape the feathers to a paper plate (the turkey's body) so that their tips extend past the outer edge of the plate and fan out next to each other, like the feathers of a real turkey.

Tape a pipe cleaner to the other side of the plate, extending it beyond the top (feathered) edge to form the turkey's neck. Bend and twist two more pipe cleaners, taping them to the bottom of the plate to make feet. Finally, cut out a round piece of construction paper for the head, gluing or taping it to the end of the neck. Have the child write the capital letter *T* twice (for *Tom Turkey*) on the turkey's "body."

140 · GIVE ME A RING

This ring-toss game makes it fun to practice one of the more difficult letters.

WHAT YOU'LL NEED: Poster board, blunt scissors, 12" to 24" pole, paper, pen

Active children can prepare to write by playing all kinds of physical games.

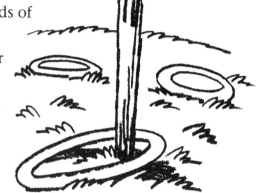

To make a ring toss game, cut several rings from poster board or cardboard. Make the hole of each ring about 6" in diameter. Put the pole in clay or sand to hold it upright. Invite the child to throw the rings around the pole. Each time he or she succeeds, have the child say the word *ring* and write the letter *R* on a scorecard. Continue until the child has scored at least five rings.

TACTILE LETTERS · 141

Here is a "sense-ational" way to learn letters.

WHAT YOU'LL NEED: Lightweight cardboard, burlap, blunt scissors, alphabet stencils, glue

Children learn by using their senses, and touching is part of such learning. This activity is very good for a young child.

Cut out 26 pieces of burlap measuring approximately 5" × 5". Make alphabet stencils and transfer the letters onto the burlap squares. Cut out the burlap letters. Glue them onto square pieces of cardboard. Make a set of capital or lowercase letters—or both. The object is for the child to close his or her eyes and feel the burlap letters, tracing the letter formations. Have the child tell you which letter it is.

Variation: Put the letters in a bag and have the child reach inside and feel the letter. Then have the child tell you what the letter is before pulling it out to see if the answer is correct.

142 BUSY BEES

▼▼▼▼▼▼▼▼▼▼▼▼▼▼▼▼▼▼▼▼▼▼▼

Paper bumblebees hold a meeting in this letter-recognition game.

WHAT YOU'LL NEED: Construction paper, blunt scissors, marker or pen

In this activity, children can learn to identify letters by manipulating paper cutouts.

Draw and cut out five construction-paper bumblebees with the child. Write the letters *A* through *E*, one letter on each bee. Ask the child to perform actions with the bees as you give instructions. For example: Put bees *C* and *D* together; have bees *A* and *E* fly away together; have bees *B*, *C*, and *E* hold a meeting.

WACKY WEEK 143

Kids can "fry fish on Friday" and "sell socks on Saturday" in this silly song activity.

Use song and pantomime to practice beginning sounds in words. Sing an "action" song about the days of the week to the tune of "Here We Go 'Round the Mulberry Bush." For example:

This is the way we wash our windows,

Wash our windows, wash our windows,

This is the way we wash our windows

So early Wednesday morning.

Have the child think of an action using words that begin with the same letter as the name of each day of the week. For example, "munch our meat on Monday" and "tickle a tiger on Tuesday." Encourage the child to pantomime each action as he or she sings the song.

SIDEWALK STEP

144

A letter patch helps teach alphabetical order one step at a time.

WHAT YOU'LL NEED: Chalk, 12 letter cards (two each with letters *A* through *F*), butcher paper or wrapping paper (optional)

Draw a path of six blocks on the sidewalk. If you wish to play indoors, make the path on a long sheet of butcher paper or the blank side of a roll of wrapping paper. Write the letters *A* through *F* in order on the path spaces.

Shuffle the letter cards and ask the child to take the first one. If the card says *A*, the child steps into the first space and puts the card on the space. If not, the child must keep drawing until he or she picks an *A*, putting unused cards at the bottom of the pile. Repeat the activity with the letters *B* through *F*. You can also repeat the game using other sets of letter cards.

145

PENCIL, CRAYON, MARKER

Here's an activity that exercises hands and minds.

WHAT YOU'LL NEED: Paper, pencil, crayon, marker

Writing with three different instruments will give children plenty of hand exercise.

In a row at the top of a sheet of paper, draw a small pencil, a crayon, and a marker. Write the letter *P* next to the pencil, *C* next to the crayon, and *M* next to the marker. Make up a sentence that contains a word that begins with *P*, *C*, or *M*. For example, you might say, "I went to the store and I saw *potatoes* (or *crackers* or *milk*)." Ask the child to use the writing tool whose name has the same beginning letter as the word to write that letter in the correct column.

ABC CUPS

146

It's sort of satisfying to put objects into their very own letter cups.

WHAT YOU'LL NEED: Marker, masking tape, three plastic drinking cups, small objects as described below

What seems like a simple sorting exercise reinforces a child's vocabulary and the ability to identify letters.

Mark three plastic drinking cups with the letters *A*, *B*, and *C* (one letter per cup) using a permanent marker and masking tape labels. Collect several small objects whose names begin with each of these letters, such as an animal cracker, toy airplane, and an acorn for the letter *A*; a ball, bandage, and bean for the letter *B*; and a playing card, piece of candy, and a cotton ball for the letter *C*.

Put the items in random order on a table, and ask the child to put each object in the cup with its beginning letter on it. Discuss the names of the objects as the child completes the activity. Repeat the activity using other letters and objects.

147

LETTER PATTERNS

Cut out paper letters, and help set a pattern for learning.

WHAT YOU'LL NEED: Poster board, paper, blunt scissors, marker or crayon

Using patterns to create letters will improve a child's dexterity.

Draw and cut out several letter shapes from poster board, such as *A*, *P*, and *T*. On a sheet of paper, write a word that can be formed from the letters, for example, *PAT* or *TAP*. Have the child arrange the letter shapes that will form the word and then trace around them with a crayon or marker to write the word.

148

WHAT WILL IT BE?

▼▼▼▼▼▼▼▼▼▼▼▼▼▼▼▼▼▼▼▼▼▼▼▼▼▼▼▼▼▼▼▼▼

Follow directions to discover the mystery object.

WHAT YOU'LL NEED: Paper, crayons

This drawing task involves giving directions to the child and seeing if he or she can follow the directions to form an object. The concepts of left to right, top to bottom, straight, and down will be reinforced.

Think of an object and give step-by-step directions to the child to create it. For example, here is how you might give directions to draw a rectangle:

1. Draw a straight line on the left side of your paper.

2. Draw a straight line on the right side of your paper.

3. Draw a straight line on the top of the paper, connecting the top of the line on the left to the top of the line on the right.

4. Draw a straight line on the bottom of the paper, connecting the bottom of the line on the left to the bottom of the line on the right.

After the child follows these directions, ask him or her what has been made. As the child's ability to follow directions grows, increase the complexity of the object to be drawn. See if you can direct the child to draw letters of the alphabet without naming them in advance.

TONGUE TWISTERS

Terrible Tommy tickled Terry's tiny toes.

No one knows Noah's nose like
Noah knows Noah's nose.

149 ·········· CLOUD PICTURES

Find a cat or a car in a cumulus cloud.

WHAT YOU'LL NEED: White chalk or crayon, blue construction paper

Looking for images in cloud formations is a great creative exercise. With a little extra effort, you can also turn it into a lesson in beginning letters.

On a day with many clouds in the sky, go outside with the child and talk about them, noting how they sometimes look like animals or objects. Take turns pointing out clouds and saying what you think they resemble.

While outside, or when you get back inside, ask the child to re-create some of the cloud objects he or she saw by drawing them with white chalk or crayon on blue construction paper. Encourage the child to describe the cloud drawings to you, then print the beginning letter of the object that the cloud resembles in the upper-right corner of the page.

PHONICS FUN FACT

Of the 20,000 common words containing the consonant *f*, only in the word *of* is the *f* pronounced irregularly (that is, like a *v* instead of an *f*).

LINES AND DOTS

150

Here's a game that adds a touch of competition to a simple connect-the-dots activity.

WHAT YOU'LL NEED: Marker or pen, sheet of paper, colored pencils or crayons (a different color for each player)

In this activity, children practice making the kind of precise strokes that are necessary to "draw" letters.

Make a grid of dots approximately one inch apart on a sheet of paper. Taking turns, each player draws a single line from one dot to another using the writing utensil with his or her assigned color. The goal for each player is to complete a square.

Take turns drawing lines and making squares until no more squares are possible. At the end of the game, use the different colors to count up how many squares each player completed.

151

LETTER SCULPTURES

The artistic shapes of the alphabet are just around the bend in this activity.

WHAT YOU'LL NEED: Clay, pipe cleaners

Simple sculpting becomes a hands-on learning experience in this engaging activity.

Help the child make a long, flat base, measuring about 3" × 12", out of clay. When that's done, ask him or her to make letter shapes out of the pipe cleaners, spelling his or her name by standing the shapes in the clay.

HOLE-PUNCHED LETTERS

*Here's a creative way of writing letters that's a
hole* lot *of fun.*

WHAT YOU'LL NEED: Blunt scissors, two sheets of white paper, marker or
pen, hole puncher, one sheet of construction paper (pick a dark or
bright color), glue

Here's an activity that engages children's hands while helping them match beginning sounds with letters and objects.

Cut the following shapes from a sheet of regular white
paper: a cup, a fish, and a boat. Write the letters *C, F,* and *B* on
a separate sheet of paper, and ask the child to tell you which
letter stands for the beginning sound in each shape's name.

Show the child how to use a hole puncher to make holes in a sheet
of paper, then instruct the child to use the hole puncher to make the
letter for the beginning sound of each object's name directly on the cup, fish, and boat shapes.
Paste each shape with its hole-punched letter on a sheet of colored construction paper.

MACARONI LETTERS

*There's no cheese, but lots of pasta, in this recipe for
hand-eye coordination.*

WHAT YOU'LL NEED: 18″ length of yarn, uncooked macaroni

Tasks such as threading pieces of macaroni on a string can help a child improve hand-eye
coordination, which is necessary for learning to read and write.

Tie a knot at the end of a length of yarn and show the child how to string macaroni on it.
When the string of macaroni is complete, tie a knot at the other end. Ask the child to make
different letters by laying the string of macaroni on a tabletop and forming letter shapes.

MYSTERY MAZE

*Go through a mystery maze to find and learn
the lowercase **m**.*

WHAT YOU'LL NEED: Paper, pen, pencil

The child learns several reading skills in this fun activity.

Design and draw a maze with a pen on a piece of paper, as illustrated in the accompanying drawing. Place a capital *M* at the start and a lowercase *m* at the end of the maze.

Ask the child to take a pencil and begin at the capital *M* and follow a path to reach the lowercase *m* at the end. The purpose of the maze is for the child to learn the lowercase *m* and to relate the letter to its sound, as in the word *maze.* In addition, by using those beginning and ending points, the child will be working through the maze going from left to right, reinforcing the directions used in the reading and writing process.

155 ON AGAIN, OFF AGAIN

Here's a way children can learn to recognize two important words.

WHAT YOU'LL NEED: Paper plates (one for game board and one for each player), paper fastener, small piece of poster board, pen or marker, six construction-paper or plastic board-game markers for each player

Play a game that teaches simple word recognition. For the game board, draw six sections on a paper plate. Write *on* or *off* in each section, alternating the words. Fasten a long spinner made out of poster board to the center of the plate with a paper fastener.

To play the game, write each player's name on a paper plate. Have the players take turns spinning the spinner. If the spinner stops at *on,* the player puts a marker on his or her plate. If the spinner stops at *off,* he or she does not get a marker. Continue until one player has six markers on his or her plate.

ALPHABET MEASURING 156

Mix one measure of counting with two measures of letter identification.

WHAT YOU'LL NEED: Measuring spoon, small container of sand (or flour), three plastic drinking cups (marked *A, B,* and *C*)

Following your specific instructions, a child can master measuring skills while learning to recognize letters.

Show the child how to dip the measuring spoon into the sand (or flour), level it, and pour it into a cup. Have the child follow your directions and put specific amounts of sand in the letter cups. For example, you might say, "Put two tablespoons of sand in the *B* cup," or, "Put three tablespoons of sand in the *C* cup." For an added challenge, add more letter cups.

RAINBOW MAKER

157

Kids won't care what's over the rainbow when they create this colorful arc out of clay.

WHAT YOU'LL NEED: Picture of a rainbow (or crayons and paper to draw one), clay or "play dough" in several different colors

Introduce a child to one of nature's wonders while contemplating the letter *R*.

Discuss rainbows with the child. Talk about a time when you saw a rainbow in the sky. Find a picture of a rainbow in a magazine or picture book, or ask the child to draw a picture of one.

Ask the child to identify the beginning sound in the word *rainbow* and say some other words with the same beginning sound. Help the child make several long coils of clay or "play dough" in several different colors. Show the child how to put the coils close together in arcs to make a rainbow.

RIDDLE TIME

What is a happy ending for a story about a lost dog?
(The hound is found.)

COMPUTER COPYCAT

158

E is for e-mail and O is for on-line when you're a child of the computer age.

WHAT YOU'LL NEED: Computer, pencil, sheet of paper

Expose a child to a device he or she will have to master some day—the computer keyboard—while he or she practices identifying and copying letters.

Show the child where letters are located on a computer keyboard. Press the "caps lock" key so that only capital letters will be displayed. Tell the child to press any letter key, then have him or her copy the letter with a pencil on a sheet of paper.

Continue by having the child press as many as five letter keys, copying the series of letters on paper. More advanced children can be directed to press specific letters to spell a word they know.

159

PIPE CLEANER LETTERS

Twisting, bending, and shaping letters is easy when you use pipe cleaners.

WHAT YOU'LL NEED: Pipe cleaners

Children love to twist and bend pipe cleaners. The challenge in this activity is to make capital and lowercase letters with them.

Initially, give the child four pipe cleaners. The child will need to think of the type and number of lines that are needed to make a particular letter. For example, the letter *M* has four straight lines (two vertical and two diagonal), while the letter *S* is one continuous curved line. Have fun and see if the child can spell his or her name using pipe cleaners.

Variation: For a challenge, see if the child can use only one pipe cleaner to make a letter.

ABC GO!

▼▼▼▼▼▼▼▼▼▼▼▼▼▼▼▼▼▼▼▼▼▼▼▼▼▼▼▼▼▼▼

160

Kids need quick hands and sharp eyes to play this fast-paced game.

WHAT YOU'LL NEED: Pad of self-adhesive notes, marker or pen

This activity is designed to sharpen a child's letter- and word-recognition skills.

Start with eight notes. Select four simple words, writing each one on two separate notes. Words to start with are *car, big, top,* and *nut.*

Give the child one set of words and keep the other set. Each player attaches one note to the front of each hand and one note to the back of each hand. Begin with the players putting their hands at their sides. One player says, "ABC Go!" and then each player displays the front or back of his or her right or left hand. The child looks at the words displayed by each player and decides whether they match. If they do, the words are removed. If they do not, the game is repeated.

Play until all notes have been paired and removed. Then new words can be written. Children with more highly developed coordination can put notes on index fingers and thumbs.

WOOD SANDING

161

Keep young hands busy going around and around, up and down, and side to side sanding wood.

WHAT YOU'LL NEED: Wood, sandpaper

Need some help with a refinishing project? Ask the child to help you and at the same time develop the small muscles necessary for writing.

Select a piece of wood. Give the child a piece of coarse sandpaper. Show the child how to sand the furniture by using different motions—circular, up and down, and back and forth. Describe these motions as they are being done. These are the same motions that are used when writing letters.

162

CHAIN OF LETTERS

Make a paper chain, and practice forming letters.

WHAT YOU'LL NEED: Construction paper, blunt scissors, glue, letter cards

In this activity, the child creates a long paper chain, which he or she can use to form any of the alphabet's letters.

Cut several strips of paper approximately 6" long. Help the child make a paper chain by gluing the first strip into a circle and then linking and gluing the strips inside one another to make a chain. When the chain is about 24" long, ask the child to lay the chain down in the shapes of letters that he or she copies from letter cards.

163 ALPHABET QUILT

No sewing is necessary in this quilting bee.

WHAT YOU'LL NEED: Marker or pen, two sheets of poster board, sheet of paper, blunt scissors, crayons or colored pencils

Because making an alphabet quilt takes time, finishing one gives a child a real sense of accomplishment. Besides reinforcing letter recognition, this activity gives a child a strong introduction to two-dimensional letters.

Draw lines to divide one sheet of poster board into 30 squares. Then write the letter *Q* and the word *quilt* on a sheet of paper. Explain that a real quilt is made of cloth; display one if available, or find a picture of one in a book or magazine. Point out that quilts have interesting patterns that are sewn on.

Tell the child that he or she will make an alphabet pattern on paper that can be used to make a cloth quilt. On another poster board, draw and cut out a pattern for each letter of the alphabet sized to fit inside the quilt squares. (Since the alphabet has only 26 letters, repeat any four letters to fill the extra squares.) Instruct the child to trace the letter patterns within the quilt squares and then color them. This can be an ongoing project if you do a few letters each day.

RIDDLE TIME

What do you call musicians on the beach? (a sand band)

164 LETTER WINDOWS

Open your window and pull in a letter.

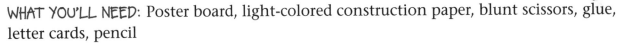

WHAT YOU'LL NEED: Poster board, light-colored construction paper, blunt scissors, glue, letter cards, pencil

Children can improve their small-muscle coordination by helping cut and paste the pieces for this activity.

Have the child help you make a house by gluing a sheet of light-colored construction paper to the poster board. Make a triangular roof out of another sheet of construction paper and glue it on top of the house shape. Draw three rows of square windows on the house, with three windows in each row. From another sheet of construction paper, cut squares the size of the house windows plus a ½" flap on top. Put glue on the flaps and glue one over each window. With a pencil, write a letter on each window (not each flap).

After the child has studied the letters on the windows, cover each one with its flap. Remove the letter cards for the nine letters you wrote on the windows and shuffle the nine cards. Have the child pick a card and then try to choose the window with the matching letter. If the child chooses correctly, he or she puts the letter card aside. If not, the child puts the card at the bottom of the card pile and goes on to the next letter card. Continue until all the letters have been correctly chosen. To play again, erase the letters on the windows and write new ones.

165 FOLDING ALPHABET

Folding fans is a fabulous way to form flexible fingers.

WHAT YOU'LL NEED: Blunt scissors, construction paper of various colors, large piece of poster board, glue

Working with colorful strips of paper can make learning letter shapes a lot more fun.

Cut construction paper into 10 strips measuring approximately 1″ × 12″ and 10 strips measuring approximately 1″ × 6″. Use a variety of different paper colors. Show the child how to fold the strips like a fan, making folds about one inch apart.

After the child has folded several strips of each size, have him or her arrange them in the shape of letters on the poster board. The child may make random letters, specific names, or begin the alphabet. The strips can be attached to the poster board with a few spots of glue. Cut more strips if the child wants to make the whole alphabet.

T PICTURE 166

Kids can cross their T's with lots of different materials in this letter collage.

WHAT YOU'LL NEED: Two drinking straws, two pieces of uncooked spaghetti, two pretzel sticks, two pipe cleaners, two Q-tips, two Popsicle sticks, glue, sheet of poster board

Common items found around the house can be arranged to make letter forms—and a work of art.

Have the child arrange each pair of objects—drinking straws, spaghetti, pretzel sticks, pipe cleaners, Q-tips, and Popsicle sticks—to make a capital or lowercase *T*. Then help the child glue each *T* onto a sheet of poster board using glue. Find a place to put your *T* picture on display.

This activity can be repeated with other capital letters that have straight lines—for example, *A, E, F, H,* and so on.

LETTER FEELINGS

167

Reach inside a grab bag to feel and identify letters.

WHAT YOU'LL NEED: Magnetic or wooden capital and/or lowercase letters, bag

This activity focuses the child's attention on the formation of letters, which is necessary for letter recognition.

Place all the capital or lowercase letters in a bag. Have the child reach inside the bag, feel a letter, and describe it so that you can guess what letter it is (for example, the letter *A* might be described as two long diagonal lines with a smaller line connecting them). Then reverse roles. You pick and describe a letter, and the child tries to guess its identity.

168

ROCK, SCISSORS, PAPER

Rock crushes scissors, scissors cut paper—but kids are the big winners in this activity.

WHAT YOU'LL NEED: Marker or pen, three index cards, small rock, sheet of paper, blunt scissors

Teach a child to distinguish between the letters *R, S,* and *P* using a classic hand game.

Write the letter *R* on one index card, *S* on another, and *P* on the third. Hold up a rock, and ask the child to identify the beginning letter in its name. Do the same with the paper and scissors.

Show the child how to play "Rock, Scissors, Paper" with your hands: Make a fist for the rock, hold up the first two fingers for the scissors, and hold the hand flat for the paper. Tell the child you will hold up a card with a letter on it. The child should respond by making the hand signal for rock, scissors, or paper, depending on which of those words begins with that letter.

 **169** # DIALING FINGERS

Little fingers that are itching to use the phone like grown-ups will be satisfied with this pretend activity.

WHAT YOU'LL NEED: Pen or pencil, paper, toy telephone with push buttons containing letters

Here's a spelling exercise that introduces a child to one of the wonders of modern technology—the telephone.

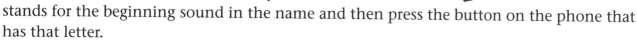

Explain to the child that, with real telephones, people must use specific numbers when they want to call someone. Tell the child that you will play a game in which he or she pretends to call friends and relatives by pressing the letters in their names instead of telephone numbers.

Ask the child to name someone, such as "David," who he or she will pretend to phone. Print the name on a piece of paper. Have the child say the letter that stands for the beginning sound in the name and then press the button on the phone that has that letter.

See if he or she can finish spelling the name this way. If not, you can help by saying the letter and having the child find and press the correct button on the telephone.

PHONICS FUN FACT

Since 1972, the *Supplement to the Oxford English Dictionary* has included more than 60,000 words.

WORD SENSE

Apple, ball, cat. Chapter 4 activities focus on simple word recognition, beginning with words for things children experience every day: foods, toys, pets, and household objects. Children can begin by visually matching words on dominoes and progress to building new words with letters and word parts printed on cards. With the activities "Rhymin' Simon" and "Rhymes from A to Z," children experiment with rhyme—word play that is also a valuable teaching aid.

WORDS ON THE GO

Try this travel word game, and make your trip a productive one.

WHAT YOU'LL NEED: Paper, pencil

Reading takes place not only at home and school, but also elsewhere within one's environment.

Make a long trip seem shorter by giving the child a piece of paper and a pencil. Whenever the child sees a word or sign that he or she can read, have him or her say the word and write it down on the paper. For example: *stop, do, not, gas, turn, go.* At the end of the trip, tally how many words were recognized. Ask the child to read the list of words aloud.

171 SUN/RAIN

Meteorologists need not apply. This activity focuses on the simple pleasures of the day's weather.

WHAT YOU'LL NEED: Paper, crayons or coloring pencils

Here's an activity that helps a child learn and compare two simple words whose meanings—and spellings—couldn't be more different.

Take the child for a walk on a sunny day, and talk about what you see. When you come in, print the word *sun* on a sheet of paper. Have the child draw a picture of the sunny day. Ask the child to think of other words that begin like *sun*. Repeat the activity on a rainy day, writing the word *rain* on a sheet of paper. Display the two pictures together, and discuss how they are alike and different.

PHONE FUN 172

Believe it or not, talking on the phone can be educational.

WHAT YOU'LL NEED: Telephone, word cards

Children will feel grown up making a telephone call to share their word skills with a friend or relative.

Review a set of word cards that the child has learned. Help the child call a favorite adult friend or relative on the telephone and read the words that he or she knows. Prepare the adult ahead of time so that he or she offers plenty of praise and encouragement.

ME WORDS

173

Use the letters in your name to describe yourself.

WHAT YOU'LL NEED: Paper, marker or pen

This activity helps to expand a child's vocabulary and grasp of beginning word sounds.

Ask the child to think of a word beginning with each letter of his or her first name. Tell the child that each word should be one that describes him or her. Using the name Cathi as an example, the child might pick the words *Cute, Adorable, Terrific, Happy,* and *Interesting.*

It can be entertaining to hear the words a child will use to describe himself or herself.

174

QUESTION DAY

Have fun asking who, what, where, when, why, and how.

WHAT YOU'LL NEED: Paper, pencil

Children are naturally curious and ask a lot of questions. Take time out and help the child write a list of questions to which he or she would like to know the answers: "When is dinner?" "Why is it raining?" "Where does a turtle live?"

Title the list "Questions I Have." Call attention to the beginning letter of the word *question.* Explain to the child that the letter *Q* will always be followed by the letter *U.*

When all the questions are written down, show him or her what is at the end of each question (a question mark). Ask the child to make a question mark. Next, point out the words that are used for asking a question (*who, what, where, why, when, how*). Have the child underline these "question words." Review the *Q* sound in the word *question.*

WEATHER CHART

175

This chart will help you keep a record of your local weather.

WHAT YOU'LL NEED: Construction paper of various colors to make weather symbols (for example, yellow to make a sun, white to make clouds, blue for raindrops), blunt scissors, monthly calendar (with the days of the week spelled out)

Children are curious about the weather: What makes it rain? Why is it sunny?

Help the child to make an assortment of weather symbols—a sun, clouds, raindrops, etc. Each day, he or she can place the appropriate weather symbol on the calendar square for that day. Have the child go outside or look out the window and observe the weather conditions. Is it sunny, cloudy, or rainy? Discuss the weather each day, then let the child select the appropriate weather symbol.

By using a calendar every day, the child will learn to recognize and read the days of the week. He or she will also learn how symbols represent words.

176

COLOR CLUES

Color your world with color names.

WHAT YOU'LL NEED: Index cards, markers of various colors

In this activity, the child learns to read the names of colors.

Print a color word *(red, blue, green)* on an index card using a marker of that color (in other words, use a red marker for *red,* blue marker for *blue,* etc.). After the child has mastered associating the words with the matching colors, make another set of word cards. This time use a black marker. See if the child can match these word cards with the appropriate color marker.

ZOO

Every child likes to act like an animal sometimes, and this game actively encourages it.

WHAT YOU'LL NEED: Sheet of paper, marker or pen

Children's natural love of animals can be channeled into wordplay that helps develop reading skills.

On a sheet of paper, print the word *ZOO* in capital letters. Ask the child to identify the first letter of the word. Say the word together several times.

Talk with the child about trips to the zoo, or zoos he or she may have seen on TV or in movies, and encourage the child to think about some of the animals he or she saw there. Whenever the child mentions a specific animal, ask him or her to identify the beginning letter of the animal's name. Make a list of all the animals the child names, then show him or her the list and say, "Can you find the ____?" Read one of the animal names on the list, and see if the child can find that word.

Variation: Take turns acting like zoo animals, such as an elephant, monkey, gorilla, lion, and bear, as the other player guesses the animal's identity and identifies the word on the list.

178 LABELING FRUIT

Here's an appealing activity using some of our favorite foods.

WHAT YOU'LL NEED: Seed catalogs, paper, glue or clear tape, blunt scissors, fruit name cards, pen or pencil

In this activity, children learn to read the names of assorted fruit with the help of their corresponding pictures.

Ask the child to find pictures of different kinds of fruit in old seed catalogs, and let him or her cut them out with blunt scissors. Glue or tape these fruit pictures in a column on the left side of a sheet of paper.

Make cards on which you print the names of the selected fruits, one fruit per card. Spread out the cards, and ask the child to place the correct card next to the picture of that fruit. Encourage the child to match the printed word to its picture by sounding out the beginning letter of the fruit word and the fruit picture.

BUILDING WORD STEPS 179

See how many words you can use to describe a single object.

A child's vocabulary and use of descriptive phrases can be enhanced with this activity.

Ask the child to say a letter (for example, *B*) and then think of an animal or object beginning with that letter (for example, *ball*). For the next step, have the child add a word that begins with *B* to further describe the ball (for example, *big ball*). Add a third step with yet another *B* word (for example, *big blue ball*). Continue with as many steps as the child is capable of making.

BIG
BIG BALL
BIG BLUE BALL
BIG BRIGHT BLUE BALL

180 ALL ABOUT ME

▼▼▼▼▼▼▼▼▼▼▼▼▼▼▼▼▼▼▼▼▼▼▼▼▼▼▼▼▼▼▼▼▼

Be an author! Here's a chance to write an autobiography.

WHAT YOU'LL NEED: Crayons, paper, yarn or O-rings, hole puncher

What better way for a child to express himself or herself than by writing a book?

Ask the child to draw a picture of himself or herself and write his or her name below the picture. Other pages to be added to the book may be about family, friends, favorite foods, toys, books, colors, or places to visit. When the child has drawn these pictures, write a caption sentence about each page; for example, "My favorite food is _____." Say the letters as you are writing so the child associates them with their sounds.

Help the child make a special cover for this book. Assemble the book by punching holes along one side of each page. Yarn or O-rings can then be used to bind the book. On the back cover, date the book. It will become a keepsake. Try making a new book every month or two to see how the child's ideas, art, and spelling ability change from one time to the next.

TALL TALES 181

▬ ▬ ▬ ▬ ▬ ▬ ▬ ▬ ▬ ▬ ▬ ▬ ▬ ▬ ▬ ▬ ▬ ▬

Weave an alphabetical tale with a group of friends.

Children put the alphabet to good use in this group activity.

Alternating turns with one or more friends or parents, the first child names a word beginning with the letter *A*, the next person picks a word beginning with a *B*, and so on. To complicate the exercise, the words should combine to tell a story. For example: *Alice Bakes Cookie Dough Every Friday.* See if you can use the entire alphabet. As the story evolves, it can be written down and read when completed.

WORD FACTORY

182

This game teaches children to construct simple words.

WHAT YOU'LL NEED: 36 blank index cards, marker or pen

Play a game similar to Scrabble that challenges a child to put letters together to make words.

Make a letter card for each letter of the alphabet. Make two extra sets of the letters *A, E, I, O,* and *U.* Give each player six cards. Work with the child to create words using as many of the six letters as possible. Have the players take turns making words. After spelling a word, a player may draw as many new cards as he or she used.

183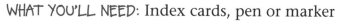

MAKING SENTENCES

Unscramble words to make sensible sentences.

WHAT YOU'LL NEED: Index cards, pen or marker

The child will actually make a complete sentence, including punctuation, in this challenging activity.

Make and then scramble word cards, each containing one of the following words: *cat, fat, mat, sat, A, on,* and *a.* Also make one card with a period (.) on it. Have the child take the cards and arrange them to make a sentence.

In this activity, attention is being called to beginning a sentence with a capital letter, ending the sentence with a period, and arranging words to make a complete thought: *A fat cat sat on a mat.* The child is using his or her knowledge of letters and sounds, combining them to make words, and then using those words to make a sentence.

DESCRIPTIVE RHYMES

184

Finding descriptive rhyming words can be a challenge.
Have fun making interesting combinations.

WHAT YOU'LL NEED: Index cards, pen or marker

In this activity, the child will learn to construct sentences using fun rhyming words.

Make a set of rhyming cards using one word per index card (for example, *bat, cat, fat, hat, mat, flat, pat, rat, sat*), and spread them out on a table. Ask the child to read the rhyming words. Next, have him or her find two words in the group that could be used together to describe something (for example, *fat cat*). See what other combinations can be made. Repeat the activity with other groups of rhyming words (for example, *tall, mall, ball, small, fall, wall, stall, call, hall*).

185

WHAT DOES IT SAY?

Every object has a name. Match words to objects
in your room.

WHAT YOU'LL NEED: Index cards, markers

After letter sounds have been mastered and the capital and lowercase letters have been learned, the next step is to apply that knowledge to reading words.

Write simple words (for example, *ball, pen, desk, cup*) on index cards. Make sure the words correspond to objects found in the child's room. Give the child a card and ask him or her to sound out the word printed on the card. When the word is said, instruct the child to take the card to his or her room, locate the object matching that word, and place the card next to the identified object.

186 REFRIGERATOR WORDS

These words will be "cool" to spell out and read.

WHAT YOU'LL NEED: Magnetic letters, index cards, pen or marker

While you are in the kitchen preparing dinner, the child can be with you constructing words on the refrigerator with magnetic letters.

Buy a set of magnetic letters and give the child a word card (an index card with, for example, the word *dog* printed on it). Have him or her find the matching magnetic letters to spell the word. Direct the child to place each magnetic letter on the refrigerator door. Have him or her say each letter and make its sound. When all the letters of the word are placed together, have the child put those sounds together to say the word.

Repeat the activity with other words. It will be fun to share this time together in the kitchen.

KNOCK-KNOCK JOKE

Knock, knock.

Who's there?

R

R who?

R you happy?

187 LETTER SCRAMBLE

Spell a word—sound by sound and letter by letter.

WHAT YOU'LL NEED: Index cards, pen or marker, picture cards

When the child has learned all of the capital and lowercase letters of the alphabet, you can help him or her take the next step in language development.

Show the child a picture card (for example, a hat), then give him or her a stack of randomly mixed index cards, each one containing one of the letters required to spell the pictured object (in this case, *T, H,* and *A*). First, have the child tell you what the object in the picture is. Then sound out each letter in the word, and have the child take the corresponding letter card and place it in the proper spelling order. Have the child say the word and spell it aloud. Continue in this manner with other picture cards.

COPYCAT WORDS 188

Copycat or oddball? Kids decide as they look at and listen to a series of words.

WHAT YOU'LL NEED: Paper, pen

In this activity, children recognize both visually and aurally whether words are the same or different.

On a sheet of paper, write a series of three words, such as *cat/can/cat*. Read the words aloud. Ask the child to circle the word that is different. Write another row of words without reading them aloud. Again, have the child circle the word that looks different. Read the words and ask the child to repeat them. Continue with other series of words, such as *pig/pig/big; dog/hog/dog; bed/red/red; pink/pink/sink; hen/ten/ten;* and *five/five/dive*.

RHYMES FROM A TO Z · · · · · · · · · · · · · · · · · 189

Z is for Zoo—and that rhymes with boo, too, and moo!

Combine rhyming skills with a review of the alphabet and beginning sounds in this game.

Display the alphabet. Point to the letter *A* and say, "*A* is for *and*." The child must name a rhyming word *(band, hand, land, sand)*. Continue with *B* is for *ball*, *C* is for *cat*, *D* is for *dig*, and so on. Challenge a more advanced child by having him or her give a letter and a word while you say a rhyme.

190 · · · RHYMIN' SIMON

▼▼▼▼▼▼▼▼▼▼▼▼▼▼▼▼▼▼▼▼▼▼▼▼▼▼▼▼

Saying the right words can earn applause in this game of rhyme recognition.

This game gets children to practice recognizing rhyming words.

Begin by saying, "Simon says clap if the words rhyme." Then say a word pair, such as *bell/well*. The child should clap because the two words rhyme. Continue with other pairs of words, not all of which will rhyme—for example, *snake/cake, cup/star, tree/see, red/bed, mop/top, book/hook, desk/chair, paper/shoe, fish/dish,* and *dip/clip*. Challenge children who master rhyme recognition to create their own rhyming and nonrhyming pairs of words. Then it will be your turn to clap.

191 WORD DOMINOES

Word matching is fun when it's done with dominoes.

WHAT YOU'LL NEED: Index cards, marker or pen

Playing a domino game gives children practice in visually matching words.

Make 10 word dominoes by placing each card horizontally and drawing a vertical line down the center. Write a simple word on either side of the line. Write each word on two different cards. Also, make cards that have the same word twice. For example, a set of cards might read *cat/dog, dog/pig, pig/ball, ball/run, run/cat, cat/cat, dog/dog, pig/pig, ball/ball*, and *run/run*.

Play the game by spreading out the cards face down. Take turns picking a card and placing it with one end or the other next to a card with a matching word. If you select a card that doesn't match any of the words displayed, put it on the bottom of the pile and select another card. Eventually, all of the cards should be connected.

WORD SHOPPING 192

Go on an educational grocery-shopping spree in this let's-pretend game.

WHAT YOU'LL NEED: Index cards, plastic or paper grocery bag, marker or pen

Familiar food names are a good starting place for learning to read words.

Using index cards, make word cards with food names such as *apple, cookie, meat, milk*, and *juice*. Have the child choose a card, and say the word together. Then invite the child to go grocery shopping. To buy a card and put it in the bag, the child must say the food name on the card.

Variation: You might also use toy food items or even real fruits and vegetables with the word cards.

193 RHYMING CIRCLES

Find some time to rhyme fun rhymes.

WHAT YOU'LL NEED: Lightweight cardboard, brad fastener, marker or pen, blunt scissors

The child will be able to learn and review new rhyming words with this activity.

Cut a circle measuring approximately 8″ in diameter from a sheet of lightweight cardboard. With a marker or pen, divide the circle into eight equal segments, as if it were a pie. At the outer edge of the circle, write a different, frequently used consonant (for example, *S, P, T, C,* etc.) in each segment. Make eight 3″ diameter circles, and on each circle write one of the following letter pairs: *at, an, in, on, un, ap, op.* Put a hole in the center of each circle. Place one of the smaller circles on top of the 8″ circle. Connect the two circles with a brad fastener.

Have the child turn the big circle and line up the different consonants with the letter pair on the smaller circle. See what words can be created by doing this. Note, however, that not all of the combinations work. Point this out to the child. Try new centers for new words.

RIDDLE TIME

Where can you take a cold swim?
(in a cool pool)

SHOPPING LIST

194

Get ready for a trip to the store by making this shopping list.

WHAT YOU'LL NEED: Food advertisements and circulars, glue or clear tape, blunt scissors, paper

Many advertisements and circulars for food appear in newspapers. This is another source of both printed words and pictures that convey meanings.

Have the child cut out pictures of items that he or she would like to buy at the grocery store. Group the foods into categories (fruits, vegetables, meats, dairy products), then paste the pictures on a sheet of paper to form a visual shopping list. Go over the list with the child. How many *F* words are there? *V* words? *M* words? *D* words? Stress healthy foods when working on this project. Use this list for the "Grocery Store Adventures" activity on page 221.

PHONICS FUN FACT

Although there are about 40 different sounds in English, there are more than 200 ways of spelling them. The long O sound can be spelled in several ways: *stow, though, doe, sew, soul,* and *beau.* The long A sound can be spelled as in *rate, main, stay, paid, freight, break, veil, ballet,* and *obey.* The SH sound can be spelled in the following ways: *shoe, sugar, special, passion, delicious, ocean, tissue, conscience, nation,* and *champagne.*

READ THE LABEL

195

Take a closer look at the words that are part of our everyday life.

WHAT YOU'LL NEED: Index cards, marker or pen, clear tape

In this activity, children learn to recognize the words that name objects they see every day.

Make word cards with the names of objects in a room. For example, in the kitchen, you might write the words *chair, table, sink, floor, stove, window.* Help the child match each card with the object it names, and tape the card to the object. Have the child walk around the room and "read" the label on each object. Try other rooms, such as the bedroom *(bed, desk, lamp, closet)* and living room *(couch, chair, TV, shelf).*

196

JACK AND JILL

Rhyme at will with Jack and Jill.

WHAT YOU'LL NEED: Paper, marker or pen

Listening to and creating rhymes helps children begin to read and spell.

Say the first two lines of the nursery rhyme "Jack and Jill." Ask the child to name the rhyming words: *Jill* and *hill.* Write *Jill* and *hill* on a sheet of paper, and help the child think of additional rhyming words by changing the beginning sound: *bill, fill, pill, spill, still, will.* Write each word, and ask the child to point out how the words are alike and different.

SPINNING WHEEL

197

Kids can increase their vocabularies by taking a spin around the playroom.

WHAT YOU'LL NEED: Construction paper, small piece of poster board, blunt scissors, paper fastener, pen or pencil

Children can use pictures to learn to read the words for their favorite toys.

On a sheet of construction paper, draw a large circle and divide it into six or eight sections. Ask the child to name several favorite toys. Write one of the toy names in each section of the circle. Have the child draw a picture in each section that matches the word.

Meanwhile, make a spinner out of heavy paper such as poster board. Attach it to the center of the circle with a paper fastener. Take turns spinning the spinner and reading the word in the section in which the spinner stops. When the child has mastered the toy words, make circles for animal words, food words, and so on.

198

TOPSY-TURVY WORDS

Use a spinning top to help youngsters recognize the letter T.

WHAT YOU'LL NEED: Toy top, index cards, marker or pen

Challenge a first- or second-grader's word recognition skills using a spinning top.

Make word cards by writing simple words that begin with the letter *T* on index cards. Words to use include *ten, tap, tag, Tom, toe, tar, tax, tent, tall, tape, tail,* and *tell.* Have the child spin the top. Hold up a card, and ask the child to read the word on the card before the top stops spinning. If the child cannot read the word cards, draw a simple picture or other hint (such as the numeral 10 for the word *ten*) on each card before the game begins.

BUILD A WORD

199

*Letters become the building blocks of words in this
letter-recognition game.*

WHAT YOU'LL NEED: Index cards, marker or pen

Putting two cards together to make a word will help children understand word construction. The following activity is geared for children in the first or second grade.

Make two sets of cards. One set has a card for each of the following consonants: *B, C, D, F, S.* The other set has a card for each of the following word endings:

at et it ob ut

an ell ip ot un

Lay the consonant cards on a table, and put the word-ending cards in a pile. Have the child take a word-ending card and put it next to each consonant card that the word ending can be combined with to make a word. Have the child read each word. Continue through the set of word-ending cards.

200

LETTER INSERTS

Turn a cat into a cot in this letter-substitution game.

WHAT YOU'LL NEED: Paper, two different-colored markers or pens

Teach children to make new words by changing one letter at a time.

On a sheet of paper, write "c__t" three times. Using a different-colored marker or pen, write the lowercase letter *a* in the blank in the first word form to make the word *cat,* and read the word with the child. Have the child explain what the word means. Write the lowercase letters *o* and *u* in the other "c__t" word forms to make the words *cot* and *cut.* Read the words together and have the child explain them. Review all three words. Then continue with new word forms such as "p__t" *(pot, pat, pet, pit)* and "h__t" *(hat, hit, hot, hut).*

READ THE PAPER

Introduce the child to the local newspaper.

WHAT YOU'LL NEED: Newspaper

This activity will make children feel grown up as they look for words in a newspaper.

Point to a word in a newspaper headline, and ask the child to find the same word somewhere else on the page. If necessary, point to the story or paragraph in which the word can be found. To begin, find proper names, since words that begin with capital letters are easier to spot. For a bigger challenge, help the child read the words that he or she finds.

WORD BUILDING BLOCKS

Show how one letter can grow into three words.

WHAT YOU'LL NEED: Paper, pen

A word square box demonstrates how to build on single letters and letter groups to make new words. This activity is best suited for children in the first or second grade.

On a sheet of paper, draw a box at least 4″ × 4″ and containing 16 squares. Show the child how to build words: Write the letter *A* in the second box from the left in the top row. In the second row, write the *A* in the second box and add a second letter to make a two-letter word—for example, *AT*. In the third row, repeat the *A* and *T* and add a third letter to make a three-letter word—for example, *RAT*. In the fourth row, repeat the *R*, *A*, and *T* and add a fourth letter to make a four-letter word—for example, *RATE*.

Continue making 16-square boxes with other letters in the top row. Help the child make new words to complete the rows in the box. Other possible progressions include *A, AN, ANT, WANT; E, BE, BEE, BEEF; I, IT, KIT, KITE;* and *O, NO, NOT, NOTE.*

203 · A STORY TO BE TOLD

Make a new story every time you "read" a picture book.

WHAT YOU'LL NEED: Picture book, paper, pencil

A child needs to be able to interpret or "read" pictures, since sight recognition of words is very limited at a young age. By looking at pictures, stories can be understood—or imagined.

Select a picture book without written text, and look at it with the child. After going through the book, ask the child if anything seemed to be missing. When the child responds that there aren't any words, suggest that you can add them and write the story together.

Ask the child to look carefully at the pictures and tell you what he or she thinks is happening. As the child is describing a picture, write his or her story on a piece of paper. Ask the child to name different beginning letter sounds of the words in his or her story. For example, if the story involves a monkey, ask the child, "What letter does the word *monkey* begin with?" You can take this even further by asking, "What does a monkey like to eat?" When the child answers "bananas," ask him or her what letter the word *bananas* begins with.

When finished, sit back and enjoy reading the whole story with the child. A new interpretation of the pictures may be made another day.

RIDDLE TIME

Who eats saltines between meals?
(a cracker snacker)

204 WORD HANG-UP

Sometimes letters and words are just hanging around.

WHAT YOU'LL NEED: Paper, old magazines, letter cards, marker or pen, clothes hanger, plastic clothespins

Help children enjoy unusual methods of putting letters together to make words.

Think of several easy words, such as *dog, cat, bird, car, jet, cup, pig,* and *boy.* While searching through old magazines, find and cut out a picture of each one. Put a clothes hanger on a doorknob. Display the first picture. Instruct the child to find the letter cards that spell the word and clip them onto the hanger with clothespins.

WHAT'S IN IT?

205

Read the packaging to learn what you'll find inside.

WHAT YOU'LL NEED: Food packages—cans, boxes, and bags

All kinds of words are found on food packaging. Select a few of those items from your food cabinet. Ask the child to try to determine what is inside the bag, box, or can. The child may be asked what kind of soup or fruit is in a particular can, what type of cereal or cookie is in a box, or what type of chip is in a bag. Ask the child to look at the lettering on the package and, using letter sounds, sound out the word.

At an early stage of reading development, the illustrations on the package can be used as clues for sounding out and recognizing the words. Before you know it, the child will be able to do a food inventory for you.

206 TIC-TAC-TOE RHYMES

Tic-tac-toe, three in a row!

WHAT YOU'LL NEED: Two sheets of drawing paper, marker or pen, crayons or coloring pencils, blunt scissors, board game markers

Here's a way to play this classic game while learning to recognize letters and rhyming words.

Make a game card by dividing a sheet of drawing paper into nine squares (three rows of three squares). Help the child draw or color the following pictures inside the squares: a hat, mouse, boy, peach, car, goose, tree, boat, and dime. Divide a second sheet of paper into nine squares. This time, the child should draw or color a cat, house, toy, beach, jar, moose, bee, coat, and lime inside the squares and then cut these squares apart with blunt scissors.

To play, shuffle the picture cards. Players take turns picking a card and matching it to a rhyming word on the game board. If a player makes a correct match, he or she puts a board game marker on the square. The first player to get three markers across, down, or on a diagonal wins the game.

PHONICS FUN FACT

The most common words in *written* English are *the, of, to, in, and, a, for, was, is,* and *that.* The most common words in *spoken* English are *the, and, I, to, of, a, you, that, in,* and *it.*

207 FREQUENT WORD SEARCH

▼▼▼▼▼▼▼▼▼▼▼▼▼▼▼▼▼▼▼▼▼▼▼▼▼▼▼▼▼▼▼▼

Kids will find that some words appear over and over and over again.

WHAT YOU'LL NEED: Word cards, crayons, magazine page with words

What words are used most frequently? This is the time for the child to find out.

Think of a word that you believe is used frequently (for example, *the*). Give the child a card with that word on it, a crayon, and a magazine page. Every time the child sees that word on the magazine page, he or she is to put a circle around it. Search the entire page. When finished, count how many times that word was used. Remind the child that the word might begin with a capital letter.

Choose another word (for example, *on*). Give the child the word card, and, using a different crayon, have him or her circle that word on the magazine page. Then count and tally. See which word was used more frequently. Try searching for and counting words that the child thinks are used a lot.

WORD PLAY
- - - - - - - - - - - - - - - - - - - -

A was an Apple Pie, B Bit it, C Cut it, D Divided it, E Enjoyed it,
F Fought for it, G Got it, H Had it, I Inspected it, J Jumped for it,
K Kept it, L Liked it, M Mourned for it, N Nodded at it, O Opened it,
P Peeped at it, Q Quartered it, R Ran for it, S Sampled it, T Took it,
U Upset it, V Viewed it, W wanted it,
XYZ all wished for a piece.

208 LITTLE WORD SEARCH

Show how little words can grow to be large ones by adding letters.

WHAT YOU'LL NEED: Paper, pen

In this activity, suitable for first- and second-grade students, children learn reading skills by recognizing a small word in a longer word.

Write a row of words. Start with a small word and then write two longer words that contain the small word. Ask the child to underline the "little" word in each longer word, then tell how the longer words are different. Encourage advanced children to read as many words as possible. Start with the following word rows:

up pup puppy

an and hand

it bit bite

jump jumped jumping

play plays replay

PICTURE RHYMES 209

Try this illustrated rhyming activity, and see what funny pictures you get.

WHAT YOU'LL NEED: Paper, marker or pen

Children enjoy nonsense rhymes, and here is a way to enhance their creativity.

Read (or recite) nonsense rhymes to the child, then ask him or her to think of an animal or person and a word that rhymes with that animal or person. Try to include both words in a phrase (for example, a *dog* with a *log*.) Draw a picture of this rhyming combination, and write the rhyming phrase at the bottom of the illustration.

210 BIRD WATCHER

"I spy a big, black crow." Children are observers of nature in this indoor/outdoor activity.

WHAT YOU'LL NEED: Marker or pen, several sheets of paper, colored pencils or crayons

Teach the child to spell *bird,* and introduce him or her to the study of these fascinating creatures.

Print the word *bird* on a sheet of paper, and have the child copy it. On a walk in the neighborhood or in a park, tell the child to watch out for birds, pointing out and describing the different ones he or she sees—for example, "a robin redbreast sitting in a tree" or "a big, gray pigeon eating crumbs on the sidewalk." Tell the child the names of any birds that you know.

At home, display the word *bird* that the child wrote. Ask the child to draw and color pictures of the birds he or she remembers from the walk.

COLOR COORDINATES 211

Crayons are the key to identifying color words in this matching activity.

WHAT YOU'LL NEED: Crayons, index cards

Children can learn to recognize color words as they work on beginning sounds.

Make word cards with the color words *red, orange, pink, tan,* and *violet.* Lay out the word cards, along with crayons representing each of the colors, in random order. Say, "I see a color that starts like the word *very,*" and have the child choose the word card and crayon that apply. (Answer: violet.) Continue with the other colors.

SOCCER IS A KICK

Young children can play an educational version of their big sisters' and brothers' favorite game.

WHAT YOU'LL NEED: Marker, kraft paper, adhesive tape, soccer ball or large ball that bounces

In this activity, children can practice their soccer skills—and learn a new word.

Make a soccer "goal" by writing the word *kick* with a marker in large letters on a piece of kraft paper measuring at least three feet by three feet. Tape the sign on a wall in a gym, basement, or recreation room.

Ask the child to identify the initial letter in the word and its beginning sound. Say the word, and have the child demonstrate the action of kicking the ball. Tell the child to stand several feet back from the *kick* sign and kick the ball toward it. Each time he or she hits the "goal," the child can shout, "Kick!"

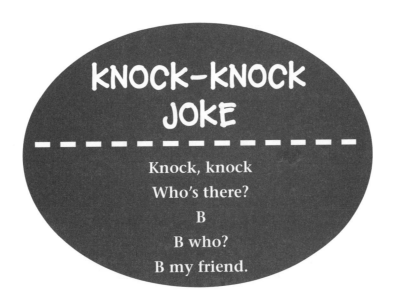

KNOCK-KNOCK JOKE

Knock, knock
Who's there?
B
B who?
B my friend.

 # WATER, WATER EVERYWHERE

A child can make quite a splash while learning the letter W.

WHAT YOU'LL NEED: Marker or pen, sheet of paper, plastic and paper cups of various sizes and shapes

This activity lets a child practice words that begin with the letter *W*. It also gives you an opportunity to discuss one of our most important natural resources.

Write the word *water* on a sheet of paper. Have the child copy the word and name other words that begin with the same sound—for example, *wash, walk, warm, worm.*

Take plastic and paper cups outside, and have the child collect water from several sources,

putting each into a different container. Possible sources include an indoor faucet, an outdoor faucet, rainwater, and pond water. Also, have the child put an ice cube from the freezer into a cup and see what happens to it.

Discuss the various sources of water and which ones contain clean or dirty water. Have the child display the water samples with the word *water* that he or she wrote, then talk about how we use water every day.

RIDDLE TIME

How do you catch a taxi?

Grab a cab.

214 · **YELLOW YES** · · · · · · · · · · · · ·

Yellow is an affirmative color in this word recognition activity.

WHAT YOU'LL NEED: Marker or pen, sheet of paper, yellow crayon, objects described below, cardboard box

Here's an activity that uses color recognition to reinforce the *Y* sound.

Print the words *yellow* and *yes* on a sheet of paper. Say the words, and ask the child to tell you how they are similar. Have the child print the word *yes* in yellow crayon, then collect several objects that are yellow. You may choose to have the child collect objects from both inside the house and outside.

Put the yellow objects in a cardboard box. Add several objects that have other colors. Pull one object at a time out of the box, and hold it up for the child to see. If it is yellow, the child has to hold up the paper with *yes* printed on it and say, "Yellow—yes."

IN, ON, UNDER ▼▼▼▼▼▼▼▼▼▼▼▼▼▼▼▼▼▼▼▼▼▼▼▼▼▼▼▼▼ 215

Get those pesky prepositions straight—and learn to read them.

WHAT YOU'LL NEED: Box, book, index cards, marker or pen

Here's a word recognition activity that will also help children understand the meaning of prepositions.

Make word cards with the words *in, on,* and *under.* Place the box on the table. Place the book on top of the box. Hold up the *on* card, and say, "The book is *on* the box." Continue by

putting the book inside the box and under the box, saying explanatory sentences and holding up the appropriate word cards. Then put the book in each position and have the child hold up the preposition card that describes its location.

216 WORD TO PICTURE

Have fun matching words to selected pictures.

WHAT YOU'LL NEED: Index cards, pen or marker, several magazines, scissors, glue or clear tape

By using letter sound skills, a child can match pictures with beginning sounds.

Find pictures of things in magazines that are familiar to the child. Cut the pictures out and glue or tape them onto index cards. Take another set of index cards and write on them the beginning letter of each object pictured.

Put the picture cards and letter cards on a table. Have the child choose a picture card and say the name of the object. Next, have him or her look at the letter cards and select the card with the same first letter as the object in the picture. Match the two cards. Later, select the letter card first, sound it out, and then ask the child to locate the matching picture.

BODY LANGUAGE 217

Kids need not look far beyond their own noses to learn to read their first words.

WHAT YOU'LL NEED: Marker or pen, index cards

Here's a phonics activity that also tests a child's quickness and coordination.

Write the words *head, neck, leg, foot,* and *toe* on separate index cards. Read each card with the child. Have the child identify the beginning sound in each word and touch the body part the word names. Shuffle the cards, and place them face down. Instruct the child to choose one card at a time, identify the body part named on the card, touch that body part, and then say another word with the same beginning sound. Remind the child to identify the initial sound in both words.

218 — HOT/COLD

*They know the sensations. Now kids can learn
to read the words.*

WHAT YOU'LL NEED: Marker or pen, 10 index cards

This simple activity teaches a child how to spell the words *hot* and *cold*.

Print the word *hot* on one card and *cold* on another. Discuss each word with the child, asking him or her to identify the initial sound in each word, as well as the other sounds if possible.

Have the child copy the word *hot* onto four more cards and the word *cold* onto four more cards. Then ask the child to put the 10 cards on items around the house (and outside, if you wish), labeling items that are either hot or cold. For example, the child might put a "hot" label on the oven door or near a fireplace and a cold label on an ice chest or wading pool.

NURSERY RHYME

Sing a song of sixpence,
A pocket full of rye;
Four and twenty blackbirds
Baked in a pie!

When the pie was opened,
The birds began to sing;
Wasn't that a dainty dish
To set before the king?

219 REBUS WRITING

Have fun writing and reading picture stories.

WHAT YOU'LL NEED: Magazines, blunt scissors, paper, glue or clear tape, pencil

As the child's ability to read emerges, try a rebus story. A rebus story combines written words that a child can read with pictures of familiar objects.

Have the child pick a topic to write about—perhaps a day at the beach. The child will say the words he or she knows and—with your help—write them down. A picture cut from a magazine is used in place of writing when the child comes to a difficult word. For example:

I went to the (picture of a beach).

I saw (picture of seashells).

I made a sand (picture of a castle).

I had fun.

Remind the child what type of letter is at the beginning of a sentence (capital letter) and what goes at the end of a sentence (period or question mark). When the story is complete, ask the child to read it back to you.

PHONICS FUN FACT

The letter of the alphabet with the highest frequency is *e*. The most frequent initial letter is *s*. The least commonly used initial letters are *q, x, y,* and *z*.

KNOCK-KNOCK!

▼▼▼▼▼▼▼▼▼▼▼▼▼▼▼▼▼▼▼▼▼▼▼▼▼▼▼▼▼▼▼▼▼

220

Here's a word-matching game that will leave even the most talkative children speechless.

WHAT YOU'LL NEED: Index cards, marker or pen

In this game, children have to give a nonverbal signal to indicate whether words they are shown are alike or different.

Make a set of word cards with simple words. Make duplicate word cards for about half the words. Explain to the child that you will play a game in which one knock signals "yes" and two knocks signal "no." Tell the child to knock on the table once to signal "yes" if you show two words that are alike and knock twice to signal "no" if they are not alike. Then show the child two word cards at a time.

221

SIGN SYMBOLS

Signs are everywhere. While traveling, identify and interpret these signs and symbols.

Next time you take an automobile trip to visit grandparents or friends, ask the child to look for traffic and advertising signs and symbols and tell you what they are. Early reading begins by interpreting various signs and symbols and associating words, sounds, and meanings to them.

One of the first signs that usually is recognized is the hexagonal STOP sign. Also look for ONE WAY, SCHOOL ZONE, NO CROSSING, and other signs and symbols during your trip. This activity expands the child's reading environment and encourages the use of beginning sounds.

ALPHABET COOKING

What child doesn't like mixing and pouring in the kitchen? Cooking is irresistible to children, and Chapter 5 shows you how to combine kitchen fun with lessons in letter sounds, letter recognition, and word recognition. Children start out making a menu based on the alphabet and end up preparing and eating just about everything they like: cookies, pancakes, crackers, and fruit. Of course, if there's anything more fun than cooking and eating food, it's "playing" with it. With "Pudding Paint" and "Soft Pretzel Letters," kids can do that, too!

222 SOUND SUPERMARKET

Cans of food can be useful for teaching beginning sounds.

WHAT YOU'LL NEED: Canned goods, grocery bag

Children love to pretend, and they love to go grocery shopping. Combine both activities. This game also reinforces children's recognition of beginning sounds.

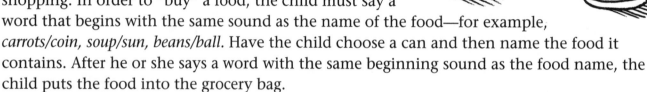

Put several cans of food on a table. Explain to the child that he or she is going to pretend to go grocery shopping. In order to "buy" a food, the child must say a word that begins with the same sound as the name of the food—for example, *carrots/coin, soup/sun, beans/ball*. Have the child choose a can and then name the food it contains. After he or she says a word with the same beginning sound as the food name, the child puts the food into the grocery bag.

At the end of the game, have the child count the cans to see how many groceries he or she has "bought." As the cans are taken out of the bag, ask him or her to say the beginning sound of the food item.

223 — POPCORN P'S

Pop some popcorn and make some P's, if you please.

WHAT YOU'LL NEED: Popcorn, popcorn popper

Make popcorn with the child. As the kernels pop, repeatedly say the word *pop*. After eating some of the popcorn, ask the child if he or she can arrange individual pieces of popcorn in the shape of the letter *P*. (For a young child, a large letter *P* can be drawn on a piece of paper, thus serving as a guide.) When the popcorn *P* has been made, write the word *popcorn* beneath it.

GELATIN ALPHABET — 224

Here's an activity that makes learning the alphabet easier to "digest."

WHAT YOU'LL NEED: Gelatin dessert mix (and listed ingredients), flat pan, letter cookie cutters, spatula, plate

In this game, children can learn their letters and eat them too!

Ask the child to help you make a gelatin dessert in any favorite flavor. Chill the gelatin in a long, flat pan. When it has solidified, use cookie cutters shaped like letters to make as many different letter shapes as possible. Use a spatula to pick up the letters and put them on a plate. Have the child name each letter before eating it. Children with more advanced reading skills can arrange the letters to spell their names or another word before they eat the letters.

ICE CREAM CONE CAKES

225

Here is a great birthday treat for a child.

WHAT YOU'LL NEED: Boxed cake mix (and listed ingredients), canned frosting, sprinkles or other toppings (optional), flat-bottom ice cream cones, hot pads, cake pan, mixer, mixing bowl, ladle

Instead of making cupcakes, try these ice cream cone cakes.

With the child's help, pick a boxed cake mix recipe and assemble all the ingredients, measuring according to the directions. Have the child put the ingredients in a bowl and stir. As you beat the mixture with a mixer, the child can place flat-bottom ice cream cones on a baking pan. Preheat your oven. Give the child a ladle and have him or her fill the ice cream cones not quite full with the mixed batter. Place the cones back on the baking pan. While the cakes are baking, decide on the frosting to be used and if any special toppings are desired when icing the cakes. Review with the child the sequence of making these cakes, and point out the long *I* sound that is heard in the words *ice cream* and *icing*.

226
BERRY DELICIOUS

*Here's a science, phonics, and nutrition lesson—
all in one small cube.*

WHAT YOU'LL NEED: Berries (blueberries, raspberries, or strawberries), ice cube tray, water or juice

Children will be fascinated by berries frozen in ice cubes in this beginning-sound activity.

Pour water or fruit juice into an ice cube tray. Have the child drop a blueberry, raspberry, or cut-up strawberry into each ice cube section. Freeze the tray. When the treats are frozen, the child can put them into a drink. Have the child explain how the ice cubes were made and then think of words that begin or sound like the word *berry*.

227 PEANUTS TO PEANUT BUTTER

Homemade peanut butter is delicious. Just shell some nuts and follow the directions.

WHAT YOU'LL NEED: Peanuts in shells, blender, vegetable oil, salt (optional), lidded jar, spatula, toast

This activity exercises the fingers and is especially good for a child with a high energy level. In addition to associating the letter *P* with peanuts, the child learns how to make peanut butter.

Give the child some unshelled peanuts, and ask him or her to crack and clean them. You may need to show the child how to crack the peanuts' shells, remove the peanuts, and skin them. When the peanuts are shelled and skinned, put a tablespoon of oil—and salt, if desired—in a blender and let the child add the peanuts. Put the lid on (only an adult should operate the blender), and process the oil and nuts. When the peanuts are blended, scoop the peanut butter from the blender with a spatula, and place it in a jar that has a lid. Have some toasted bread ready to taste this delicious treat. Refrigerate the leftover peanut butter when finished.

Variation: You and the child can make a label to put on the jar. Use a piece of paper, crayons or markers, and clear tape.

RIDDLE TIME

What do you call a swine's dance?
A pig jig

POPSICLES, PLEASE

228

On a hot day, there's nothing as refreshing as this special treat.

WHAT YOU'LL NEED: Small paper cups, fruit juice, plastic spoons or Popsicle sticks, measuring cup

Most children will enjoy helping out in the kitchen, especially if you're preparing something they like. In this activity, the child will make his or her own Popsicles.

Let the child decide what flavor of Popsicles is desired, then pour the selected juice into a measuring cup, which will be easier for the child to control. Ask the child to pour the juice into small paper cups, but only about three-fourths full. Place these cups in the freezer until the liquid begins to freeze slightly. At that point, remove the cups from the freezer and have the child push a Popsicle stick or plastic spoon (handle end out) into the thickened liquid. Put the cups back in the freezer.

After the juice has frozen completely, it's time for a taste test. Peel the paper cup from the Popsicle. As you and the child enjoy your snack, review all of the *P* words in this project: *Popsicles, please, pour, place, push, peel, plastic, put, paper.*

229

THAT'S CHEESY!

You can eat the letters in this tasty alphabet game.

WHAT YOU'LL NEED: American cheese slices or block of cheese, knife

In this activity, children can make letters out of cheese strips or sticks.

Cut slices of American cheese into strips, or slice a block of any firm cheese such as mild cheddar, mozzarella, or Monterey Jack into sticks. (Be careful with the knife around the child.) Make the sticks approximately two inches long and ½ inch wide. Have the child wash his or her hands, then show him or her how to form the cheese sticks into letters. Start with letters that are easier to form, such as *E, F, H,* and *L.* Have the child form and identify several letters before eating them.

230 CREAMY CREATIONS

Let luscious letters add pizzazz to an ordinary dessert.

WHAT YOU'LL NEED: Long pan, gelatin dessert mix (and listed ingredients), can of whipped cream

Children will have fun watching you form letters using a can of whipped cream.

First, invite the child to help you mix the ingredients to make a gelatin dessert. Put the gelatin in a long, wide pan and chill. When the dessert is ready, write letters on it with the whipped cream. Talk about the formation of each letter as you slowly make it. Have the child name each letter and give a word that begins with that letter.

FLOUR POWER 231

All you need is flour in this recipe for learning letters.

WHAT YOU'LL NEED: Cookie sheet, flour, paper, marker or pen

Use a common kitchen staple in a unique version of finger painting.

Spread flour on a cookie sheet so that the entire surface is covered with approximately ⅛" to ¼" of flour. Show the child how to print letters in the flour using an index finger. Then select one letter and write both the capital and lowercase forms of the letter (for example, *Bb*) in the flour. Have the child write the letters on paper and then draw pictures of items whose names begin with the letter (ball, bat, bird, bell, bed).

232 SOFT PRETZEL LETTERS

Twist some dough to make letters—and pretzels.

WHAT YOU'LL NEED: Measuring cups, water, sugar, salt, one packet yeast, mixing bowl, big spoon, flour, baking sheet, aluminum foil, egg, pastry brush, kosher salt

Measuring, stirring, mixing, and kneading are the procedures the child will use to make soft pretzels. These tasks can be fun for a child, and the result will be something that he or she will enjoy eating.

With the child's help, measure 1½ cups of warm water, one tablespoon of sugar, one teaspoon of salt, and one packet of yeast. Ask the child to pour the ingredients into a mixing bowl and stir. Add four cups of flour to the other ingredients and mix thoroughly.

The child can remove the dough from the bowl and knead it on a floured tabletop. Kneading the dough until it is smooth, the child will be using all of his or her hand and finger muscles. As the child is kneading the dough, discuss the different possible types of pretzel shapes you could make.

When the kneading is completed, pull off a piece of dough and shape it to make several letters (perhaps the initials of the child's name). Place these shapes on a baking sheet lined with aluminum foil. Brush the pretzel letters with a beaten egg and sprinkle with coarse kosher salt. Bake the letters at 425 degrees for 12 to 15 minutes, or until they are golden brown. Let cool before eating.

Exercise proper safety around the stove. Do not allow the child to come in contact with the heated baking sheet.

PLEASE PASS THE PANCAKES · 233

It doesn't take much to make eating pancakes a learning experience.

WHAT YOU'LL NEED: Pancake mix (and listed ingredients), mixing bowl, spoon, blueberries, pan, spatula

Here's an easy way to help children learn letters as they have fun preparing breakfast.

Pour some pancake batter into a pan. (A large pancake will give the child more space to write on.) Have the child arrange blueberries in the shape of a letter on the pancake. The child might make one of his or her initials or another favorite letter. In place of blueberries, you could use other kinds of small berries or diced fruits, such as strawberries, peaches, or apples.

234 GOING CRACKERS

There's a whole menagerie of creatures—and sounds—in a box of animal crackers.

WHAT YOU'LL NEED: Box of animal crackers, paper, marker or pen

In this activity, children practice both sorting and identifying beginning sounds.

Have the child put animal crackers into groups according to kind of animal. Then ask him or her to identify each kind of animal and say the letter that stands for the beginning sound in its name. Have the child write each beginning letter on a sheet of paper, or write each letter yourself and have the child copy it. Finally, have the child place each animal cracker on the paper next to the beginning letter of its name.

ALPHABET NOODLES

235

What letters are most frequently found in a box of alphabet noodles? Try this activity and find out.

WHAT YOU'LL NEED: Box of alphabet noodles, bowl

When grocery shopping, go down the pasta aisle. Select a box of alphabet noodles. Many phonics activities can be done with them.

In this particular activity, empty the alphabet noodles into a bowl. Have the child group the noodles by letter (all of the *A*'s, *B*'s, *C*'s, and so on). When this task is completed, help the child determine whether any letters of the alphabet are missing, which letters are the most common, and so on.

236

COOKIE CORNER

Here's an educational way to enjoy a batch of fresh-baked cookies.

WHAT YOU'LL NEED: Cookie dough, letter cookie cutters, baking sheet, decorative icing in tubes

Children can learn about letters as they eat their favorite snack.

Ask the child to help you mix a batch of cookie dough. Cookie dough from a mix, frozen dough, or refrigerated rolls of dough work just as well. Roll the dough out. Have the child use cookie cutters shaped like letters to cut the dough. After baking and cooling the cookies, help the child decorate each cookie by tracing the shape of each letter with decorative frosting in a tube.

Put the cookie letters out on a plate. Play an easy game of "I Spy," taking turns giving clues, such as, "I spy a letter that begins the word *apple*." Each cookie letter may be eaten after it has been correctly identified.

237 FRESH LEMONADE

▼▼▼▼▼▼▼▼▼▼▼▼▼▼▼▼▼▼▼▼▼▼▼▼▼▼▼▼▼

Nothing tastes better than a glass of fresh lemonade you make together.

WHAT YOU'LL NEED: Two lemons, juicer, knife, spoon, water, measuring cup, one cup of sugar, half-gallon pitcher

On a warm summer day, nothing is better than a glass of freshly squeezed lemonade. The squeezing, stirring, and pouring of the ingredients provide great muscle-developing skills.

Cut the lemons in half, and ask the child to place each lemon half on top of the juicer and squeeze it. You may need to place the juicer over a small bowl so the child can work more easily. As the child is squeezing the lemons, talk about what sound he or she hears in the beginning sound of the word *lemon*.

After the lemons have been squeezed, empty the juice into a pitcher. Help the child measure one cup of sugar and pour it into the pitcher. Stir the lemon juice and sugar. Add cold water and ice cubes to fill the pitcher. Ask the child to describe how the beverage was made, then enjoy fresh glasses of lemonade.

TONGUE TWISTERS
- - - - - - - - - - - - - - - -

Will Wanda Walrus wash Willy Weasel's wagon with warm water?

Harry hired half a herd of heavy hippos to hum harmonicas on Halloween.

238 · · · · · · · · · · · LOVABLE LOLLIPOPS

Learn about **L** *words while you make some lovely lollipops.*

WHAT YOU'LL NEED: Sugar, water, light corn syrup, saucepan, candy thermometer, wax paper, paper lollipop sticks, margarine, ladle, coloring if desired, measuring cups

What could be better than a lovely homemade lollipop? Follow this simple recipe, exercising due caution when working around the stove. Note that all cooking and handling of hot foods should be done by an adult.

With the child's help, put 2½ cups of sugar, ½ cup of water, and one cup of light corn syrup into a saucepan. Ask the child to stir this mixture until blended. Place a candy thermometer into the saucepan. Stir this mixture over medium heat until it boils and the thermometer reaches 280 degrees. While doing so, the child can prepare the wax paper. Have him or her lightly grease the wax paper with margarine and then place the lollipop sticks on the paper. Make sure that the sticks are not too close to each other.

While both of you are working, talk about the different *L* words that appear in this activity: *lollipop, liquid, light, lightly, lovable, lovely, ladle, luscious.* When the temperature of 280 degrees is reached, remove the liquid from the heat and add color if desired. Using a ladle, pour the mixture over the tops of the sticks on the greased wax paper. Let cool, and then enjoy a lollipop.

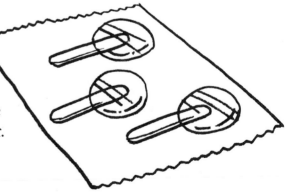

PHONICS FUN FACT

The letter *y* can be either a consonant or a vowel.
In *year*, it's a consonant.
In *happy*, it's a vowel.

239 — CARROT CONVERSATION

Here's an activity to brighten kids' eyes and polish their sound skills.

WHAT YOU'LL NEED: Carrots, carrot peeler, paper, marker or pen

While children are enjoying a healthy snack, they can practice beginning sounds.

Use the carrot peeler to make thin, curly carrot slices. As the child munches on the carrot curls, take turns saying words that have the same beginning sound as the word *carrot: cat, car, corn, can, come, kitten, kite, kettle, keep.*

For more advanced children, write the letters *C* and *K*, and point out that both letters can stand for the beginning sound in *carrot.* Then write each word that you named under the appropriate beginning letter.

FRUITFUL FUN

240

Children learn the names of fruits in this mouth-watering activity.

WHAT YOU'LL NEED: Various fruits, package of fruit string (available at grocery stores)

In this activity, children review fruit names as they work on beginning letters.

Name a fruit, such as an apple, and hold up a real apple. Have the child form the fruit string into the shape of the letter *A* for the word's beginning sound. Take turns naming other fruits, such as a banana, peach, pear, watermelon, apricot, cantaloupe, nectarine, orange, and berries. Start with common fruits, and hold up examples of each. For an added challenge, have the child describe each fruit as it is named, or give clues for each fruit instead of naming it.

241 HAMBURGER HELPER

Add some educational ingredients to your next hamburger meal; kids will relish it.

WHAT YOU'LL NEED: Ground meat, buns, other items used to make a hamburger meal

Helping with a hamburger meal is a great way for children to learn not only the steps in meal preparation, but beginning sounds in words as well.

Have the child help you prepare a meal of hamburgers, starting with making the patties. As the two of you work, discuss each food item you are using: meat, salt, pepper, bun, mustard, ketchup, pickles, beans, potato chips, and so on. Have the child name other words that begin with the same sound as the name of each food item. Using the word *meat*, for example, the child might respond with the words *map, man, mouse, make,* or *mind.*

PRETZEL PRACTICE 242

Pretzel sticks can provide a great impromptu lesson on letter formation.

WHAT YOU'LL NEED: Pretzel sticks

Not only are pretzels a tasty snack, but children can use them to form letters without making a mess.

Ask the child to wash his or her hands, then show him or her how to use pretzel sticks to form letters, including breaking them in half to form some letter parts. Start with simple stick letters such as *E, I,* and *T.* You might progress to making all the letters in the alphabet. Say each letter as the child makes it, and also have him or her name each letter frequently.

PUMPKIN PIE

Here's the best kind of recipe for kids—simple, healthy, and delicious.

WHAT YOU'LL NEED: Colored pencils or crayons, drawing paper, pie plate, pie crust, can of pumpkin and other ingredients for pumpkin pie

Have fun with the letter *P*—and reward yourselves with some pumpkin pie.

Ask the child to draw and color a picture of a pumpkin. Ask him or her to identify the beginning sound of the word *pumpkin*. Show the child how to write the letter *P* on his or her drawing.

Explain that a pumpkin pie can be made with pumpkin from a can. Prepare a frozen, refrigerated, or homemade pie crust. Show the child a pumpkin pie recipe (most cans of pumpkin include one on the label), and go through each step together. Let the child help add ingredients and mix the pumpkin pie filling.

NURSERY RHYME

What says the little duck with a yellow back?
The little yellow duck says quack, quack, quack.
What says the friendly brown cow when she looks at you?
The friendly brown cow says moo-moo-moo.
Does your calico kitten say bow-wow-wow?
No, your calico kitten
says meow-meow-meow.

SOUP'S ON!

244

A hot phonics lesson will have kids saying,
"Mm, mm, good!"

WHAT YOU'LL NEED: Can of soup, pot, bowl, spoon

Here's an activity that teaches children important kitchen skills while helping them recognize beginning sounds.

Invite the child to choose a kind of soup to prepare. Read the directions aloud, and have the child help you follow each step. While you both eat the soup, give clues to a word that begins like the word *soup,* and have the child guess the word. For example: "This is something to eat for lunch. It is made with bread." (Answer: sandwich.) Then have him or her think of another word that begins with *S* and give you clues about it.

245

VANILLA PUDDING

V stands for vegetable—but also for this very tempting treat.

WHAT YOU'LL NEED: Pen or pencil, piece of paper, box of instant vanilla pudding, milk, mixer, bowls, spoons

Children can practice their *V* sounds while helping you make (and eat) vanilla pudding.

Print the letter *V* on a piece of paper. Ask the child to think of words that begin with that letter, naming *vanilla* if he or she doesn't. Make some vanilla pudding, having the child help you follow the directions on the box and mix the ingredients.

As you are eating the pudding, discuss other words that begin with the *V* sound, such as *vacuum cleaner, valentine,* and *vitamin.* Have the child display as many of these items as possible, or write the letter *V* on sticky notes and label each item.

246 MINI-PIZZA RECIPE

Try these delicious little pizzas for lunch and learning.

WHAT YOU'LL NEED: Tomato sauce, English muffins, shredded mozzarella cheese, vegetable toppings (if desired), spoon, baking sheet, paper, crayons

Not sure what to make for lunch? How about mini-pizzas? Preheat your oven to 425 degrees, and place the ingredients on a table or counter.

First, split a muffin in half, and place the halves on a baking sheet. (You can toast the muffin first, if you want a crunchy crust.) Show the child how to spoon tomato sauce onto the muffins, followed by any vegetable toppings that he or she may like—onions and mushrooms, for example. Let the child put the cheese on the pizzas, then bake them for 10 to 15 minutes. As always, be careful that the child doesn't come into contact with the stove or heated baking pan.

While the pizzas are baking, help the child make a recipe card using pictures and beginning letters. Arrange them sequentially to show how the mini-pizzas were made. For example:

1. Picture of a muffin and the letter *M*.

2. Picture of sauce on a muffin half and the letter *S*.

3. Picture of vegetable toppings, if used, along with their beginning letters.

4. Picture of cheese and the letters *Ch*.

SWEET OR SOUR?   **247**

Kids must get their taste buds working for this savory experience.

WHAT YOU'LL NEED: Snack foods as described below

Show your good taste as you help a child review words that begin with the letter *S*.

Have the child taste several different food items and describe their tastes with an *S* word. Explain that many different kinds of tastes can be described with *S* words, such as *sweet*, *sour*, *spicy*, *salty*, *sticky*, and *sugary*. The word *soft* can also describe foods.

Prepare some snacks from among the following: potato chips, dill pickle, sweet pickle, salsa, white bread with peanut butter, pretzel, white bread with jelly, hot dog, or salami. The child can also taste lemon juice and other juices. Have the child taste each food and use one or more *S* words to describe it.

248   FAVORITE FOOD FILE

Get your recipe file in order (alphabetical order) in this activity.

WHAT YOU'LL NEED: Index cards, pen or pencil

Use an alphabetical theme to make a recipe file of children's favorite foods.

Start by asking the child, "What's your favorite food that starts with *P*?" Write a recipe card for the child's response. Point out the name of the recipe (for example, "Pepperoni Pizza"), and then discuss the steps of the recipe as you write them. Some children may wish to point out the letter *P* wherever it appears in the recipe. Continue with other letters such as *B*, *H*, *S*, *T*, and *M*.

249 CHOCOLATE LEAVES

Turn over a new leaf, and learn about the letter L.

WHAT YOU'LL NEED: Chocolate chips or bars, mint leaves bought at grocery store, double boiler, water, food brush

Children can work on beginning word sounds as they make and eat a beautiful and delicious treat.

Wash the mint leaves well. Melt some chocolate, either chips or bars, in the double boiler over boiling water, keeping the child at a safe distance from heat sources. When the chocolate has melted, use a food brush to coat the underside of each leaf with a layer of chocolate. Do not make the chocolate layer too thin, or else it will be difficult to peel off.

Put the leaves in the freezer for a few minutes to harden. Then carefully peel off each leaf. As you eat the chocolate "leaves," take turns naming other words that begin with the letter *L*.

TONGUE TWISTERS

Dandy Dog danced all day with Daisy the delicate duck.

Singing Sally sang sweet songs softly on Saturday.

250 TOUCHABLE FRUIT SALAD

Making fruit salad can be a touching experience.

WHAT YOU'LL NEED: Fruits as described below, scarf for blindfold, large bowl, knife, cutting board

Help a child master beginning letters while making a healthy snack that both of you can enjoy.

Collect as many of these fresh fruits as possible: apple, orange, grapes, pineapple, cantaloupe, peach, grapefruit, and banana. Have the child put on a blindfold, feel each fruit, and guess what it is. After each fruit is named correctly, take the blindfold off. Ask him or her to say another word that begins with the same sound as the name of the fruit.

Then ask the child to help you prepare each fruit for a fruit salad. Have the child do as many steps as is safely possible, such as washing fruit, peeling the banana, and pulling grapes from their stems. Discuss the other steps, such as cutting up the fruits, as you do them.

INITIAL SANDWICHES 251

Kids get to personalize these sandwiches in more ways than one.

WHAT YOU'LL NEED: Bagel, two slices of bread, bread knife, toppings (such as cream cheese, peanut butter, mustard, cut-up bits of ham, turkey, lettuce)

Teach a child his or her initials while preparing sandwich treats.

Toast two bagel halves and two slices of bread. Cut each bagel half into quarters, then cut each slice of toast into four strips. Lay out the curves and strips along with toppings.

Ask the child to use bagel and toast pieces to form the initials of his or her first and last names on a paper plate. Let the child top each bread bit with various ingredients.

PUGGING PAINT

252

Here's a way to write that's a little messy, but delicious.

WHAT YOU'LL NEED: Instant pudding, milk, mixer, bowl, big spoon, plastic plates

What child can resist an activity that encourages putting his or her fingers in food?

Stress the importance of clean hands when working with food items. Then have the child help you mix a package of instant pudding. (Chocolate or another dark pudding works well.) Read the directions, and discuss each step. Spread a layer of pudding on a large plastic plate. Show the child how to finger paint in the pudding. Name several letters for the child to write, or write some on paper for him or her to copy. The child may also wish to write his or her name.

253

CARROT COINS

Carrots are the coin of choice in this counting and beginning-sound activity.

WHAT YOU'LL NEED: Carrots, knife, household items described below

Children will enjoy pretending to buy things with carrot coins.

Make the coins by slicing carrots into thin, round slices. Ask the child to help you think of— and gather—household items whose names begin with the same sound as the word *carrot*. For example, you might collect a cup, a can, corn, coffee, a toy car, a candle, and a

camera. Have the child name the item he or she wishes to purchase. Give a price in carrot coins. Have the child count out the appropriate number of carrot coins.

254 ········· BANANA BOATS ·············

Kids can navigate the beginning B sound with these yummy snacks.

WHAT YOU'LL NEED: White bread, peanut butter, banana, pretzel sticks, butter knife

Children can have fun helping with each step of this fun and simple recipe, which includes a review of *B* words.

First, spread peanut butter on a slice of bread. Slice a banana lengthwise, and place one half in the center of the bread. Fold the sides of the bread up to make a boat. Fasten the boat by poking three or four pretzel sticks through both sides of the bread on top. Have the child name words that begin like *banana boat*.

MAKE A MENU ━ ▪ ━ ▪ ━ ▪ ━ ▪ ━ 255

What goes with chicken and chili? In this game, cheddar cheese.

WHAT YOU'LL NEED: Seven paper plates, canned goods, blunt scissors, marker or pen

This activity allows children to help plan lunch menus as they review beginning sounds.

Put seven paper plates in a row. Write a day of the week on each plate. Invite the child to help you plan a week's worth of lunch menus by planning each day's menu around a different beginning sound. To illustrate each menu, have the child find canned goods and boxed goods in the kitchen, or find and cut out pictures of food. For example, you might start with the beginning sound *M* (macaroni, meat, milk). The child might find a box of macaroni and cheese and cut out a picture of a glass of milk. Other menu letters are *S* (soup, sandwich), *T* (tuna, toast, tomatoes), *P* (peanut butter, pear, potato salad), *H* (hot dog, hamburger), *B* (banana, beans), and *F* (fish).

256 ALPHABET SALAD

If you've never had a radish and jalapeño pepper salad, try this recipe.

WHAT YOU'LL NEED: Letter cards containing the letters *A* through *T*, box or bowl, various vegetables, pen or pencil, paper

This activity tests a child's memory as well as his or her vocabulary.

Put the letter cards in a box or bowl, and mix them up. Ask the child to choose seven letters and name each one. Then have him or her name vegetables that could be put into a salad whose name begins with each letter. Point out that some letters may have several items and others may have none. You can also help name items for difficult letters.

Keep the following ingredients in mind: asparagus, avocado, beans, broccoli, cabbage, celery, cucumber, carrots, garlic, green pepper, jalapeño pepper, lettuce, mushrooms, olives, onions, parsley, peas, red pepper, radish, spinach, and tomato. You may also suggest other salad items, such as apples, eggs, and nuts.

Write down each vegetable the child names. Edit the list together, choosing several items for a real salad. Shop for the items together. Discuss each vegetable as you prepare it and add it to the salad.

RIDDLE TIME

What does a full moon make?
A bright night

TOOL TIME

Every good cook knows the importance of using the right utensils.

WHAT YOU'LL NEED: Ingredients and utensils needed for baking cookies, baking pan, concentrated juice drink, water, strawberries or apple slices, rotary eggbeater, spatula, plates, tongs

Snack preparation helps a child develop small motor skills through the use of kitchen tools. Explain that you will prepare a snack that requires the use of several different kitchen tools.

First, prepare a refrigerated cookie dough roll or make cookie dough using a mix or recipe. While the cookies are baking, let the child use a rotary eggbeater to mix water with concentrated juice mix.

When the cookies are done, remove them from the pan and place them onto plates, using a spatula. Then let the child add a strawberry or apple slice to the plates using tongs. Discuss all the steps, utensils, and ingredients involved in making the snack, emphasizing the beginning sounds of each.

PHONICS FUN FACT

A syllable is a word or part of a word pronounced with a single vocal sound. Each syllable must have a vowel, but not necessarily a consonant.

I LIKE ICE CREAM

258

A tasty homemade treat helps children put the I in the alphabet.

WHAT YOU'LL NEED: Large bowl, eggbeater, measuring cups, egg substitute, sugar, vanilla extract, salt, evaporated milk, whole milk

Children can consider the long *I* sound as they help make homemade ice cream. Discuss the following steps as you and the child work together.

Pour enough egg substitute to equal four eggs in a large bowl. Beat in 1¾ cups of sugar, 1½ teaspoons of vanilla extract, and ¼ teaspoon of salt. Add one cup of evaporated milk and one quart of whole milk. Stir. Place the mixture in the refrigerator until ready to freeze.

Ask the child to think of additional words beginning with the long *I* sound, such as *idea, icicle,* and *ivy,* as you work. You can also emphasize the beginning sounds of *vanilla, salt,* and *milk* as you mix the ice cream.

259

CEREAL TIME

Hot cereal can be both nutritious and educational.

WHAT YOU'LL NEED: Hot cereal mix, milk or water, bowls, spoons

Practice beginning sounds as you make a hot breakfast with the child.

Use any hot cereal mix. Microwaving the cereal allows the child to participate in all steps. Follow and discuss each step together. As you prepare the cereal, ask the child to name words that begin like cereal *(ceiling, city, celery, circus)* or oatmeal *(open, okay, over)*. Cereals may also have flavors such as cinnamon, peach, and maple syrup that can provide beginning-sound practice.

ALPHABET ARTS & CRAFTS

Tap children's creative instincts to help them explore the way letters sound and look. Chapter 6 activities challenge children to create artwork using a variety of materials such as clay, sponge paint, collage, and pipe cleaners. At the same time, they practice recognizing letters both visually and aurally and creating new words. Among the many suggestions for artwork are several items of wearable art, including "Letter Necklace" and "Letter Headband."

SOCK PUPPETS

260

Have one unmatched sock left over when your laundry is done? Put that lonely sock to use.

WHAT YOU'LL NEED: Sock, yarn, scraps of fabric, blunt scissors, marker, buttons, cardboard, glue

Have you ever finished the laundry and found that you had only one sock? What can you do with one sock?

Give it to a child, and help him or her make a sock puppet. Ask the child to think about what kind of puppet character he or she wants. Using different scraps of yarn and fabric, help the child cut out hair, scarves, a tie, or whatever is required for this special puppet. A marker or buttons can be used to make the eyes. Place a narrow strip of cardboard inside the sock before gluing objects to it. This prevents the glue from seeping through to the inside.

After the puppet is finished and the glue has dried, have a puppet show. Oral communication is very important in a young child's language development. For children who are shy, this provides an opportunity to speak through another object.

261 # BIG BUBBLES

Bubbles are fascinating—and you can learn something from them.

WHAT YOU'LL NEED: Plastic bowl, water, liquid detergent, food coloring, straws, white paper

To demonstrate comparison words and the sounds of word endings *er* and *est,* try making bubbles to show the concepts of big, bigger, and biggest.

Take a medium-sized plastic bowl and fill it three-fourths full with water. Add a small amount of liquid detergent and food coloring. Demonstrate the fine art of blowing bubbles by putting one end of a straw into the liquid and blowing gently into the other end. Then have the child try it.

Have the child blow a bubble, then a bigger bubble, and, finally, the biggest bubble he or she can make. As the bubbles appear at the top of or over the container, take a piece of paper, put it over the container, and make an instant print of the bubble. If you use different colors or bubble mixtures, you can add those bubble prints to the same sheet of paper. When finished, look at the bubble prints with the child. Ask him or her to show you the big, bigger, and biggest bubbles.

 # FINGER PAINT DESIGNS **262**

Try your hand at finger painting, and see what you can make.

WHAT YOU'LL NEED: Finger paint, paper

Set up some finger paints, and have the child experiment with different hand and finger motions, such as making swirls, straight lines, curved lines, zig-zag lines, circles, half circles, and spirals. These motions mirror the ones that will be needed for writing.

WHERE DID THEY GO?

● **263**

*Paint letters with water on a sunny day,
then see what happens.*

WHAT YOU'LL NEED: Water, container, paintbrush

What happens on a sunny day when there's water on the sidewalk? Let the child find out.

On a bright, warm day, take the child outside. Give him or her a paintbrush and a container partly filled with water. Find a safe and sunny cement surface (such as the sidewalk), and have the child "paint" letters of the alphabet. The child will be amazed at how quickly the letters disappear.

264 # NOODLE NECKLACE

▼ ▼

Try a new look with a beautiful noodle necklace.

WHAT YOU'LL NEED: Long elastic string, noodles (rigatoni, ziti). For colored noodles: food coloring, sealable plastic bag, rubbing alcohol, newspaper

With this activity, the child will associate the *N* sound with two *N* words: *noodles* and *necklace*.

Give the child an elastic string with one end knotted. Spread some noodles on the table, then have the child take a noodle and thread the elastic string through it. When enough noodles have been added, ask the child what *N* word this could be. If you need to give a clue, take the necklace, tie the ends together, and put it over the child's head.

To make colored noodles, place noodles into a sealable plastic bag, along with a small amount of food coloring and rubbing alcohol (the alcohol sets the color). Seal the bag tightly, and have the child shake the bag to coat and color the noodles. When that's done, dump the noodles onto a sheet of newspaper to dry before giving the child the knotted elastic string.

265 APPLE STAR PRINTS

What's inside an apple? Just seeds? Try this activity and you'll be surprised.

WHAT YOU'LL NEED: Apple, knife, washable tempera paint, paper towel, clean Styrofoam meat tray, paper, pen or marker

The child will learn the short vowel *A* in this arts and crafts activity.

Cut an apple in half, making the cut parallel to the stem. Ask the child to examine both halves of the apple. Point out how the exposed seed formation at the apple's core is in the shape of a star. Remove the seeds, and have the child dip the inner (skinless) side of the apple into a shallow tray of tempera paint. (This works best if a small amount of paint is put on a wet paper towel placed on a Styrofoam meat tray.)

After the paint is applied to the apple, help the child print several "stars" on white paper. As the child is making these prints, have him or her say the word *apple.* When the prints are finished, label the picture "Apple Stars." Point to the letter *A* in the word *Apple* to make the connection between the printed letter and its correct sound.

NURSERY RHYME

Tick, tock, tick, tock,
happily sings
Grandfather clock.
It's time for work,

it's time for play.
Tick, tock, tick, tock,
Grandfather clock
sings all day.

266 WHAT CAN IT BE?

A letter can be used to form many things.
See what you can make.

WHAT YOU'LL NEED: Crayons or markers, paper

It's good to stimulate a child's creativity. Here's one good way to do it.

Draw a large letter (capital or lowercase) on a piece of paper. Ask the child to create an object based on the letter's shape (for example, the letter *O* can be made into a wheel, the letter *V* into an ice cream cone). Label the drawing. See how many objects the child can create with different letters. When the project is completed, show the drawings to other family members to see if they can find the letter.

LETTER PUZZLES 267

The alphabet won't seem so puzzling to children
who master this activity.

WHAT YOU'LL NEED: Heavy paper or poster board, colored markers or crayons, blunt scissors

A letter puzzle can help children improve hand-eye coordination as they learn letter recognition.

Write two or more letters on a piece of heavy paper or poster board. Make the letters two-dimensional; in other words, draw each letter in outline form, letting the child color the inside portion of the letters. Cut the paper into several puzzle pieces. Have the child put the puzzle together and name each letter. You can make increasingly difficult puzzles, eventually using the entire alphabet.

268 ..... INGENIOUS INVENTOR

Be creative! Design a new invention.

WHAT YOU'LL NEED: Collection of scrap items

New products are added to the market practically every day, but what might a child like to create?

Emphasizing the sound of the short *I*, have the child pretend to be an inventor. Talk about what an invention is and what items in the home have been invented. Discuss how those inventions have helped us.

Give the child a collection of scrap items and see what "invention" he or she can create. When the invention is finished, talk about it. What is it? How does one use it? What will it do? How will it help us?

LACY LETTERS 269

Letters of the alphabet get ruffled in this fun art project.

WHAT YOU'LL NEED: Poster board, pen or pencil, blunt scissors, tissue paper, glue

Children will be delighted with this easy, pretty way to decorate letters.

First, outline and cut out a letter from poster board. Next, cut squares of white or variously colored tissue paper. Make each square approximately 1" × 1". Show the child how to put a square of tissue paper over a finger and then cup it around the finger to form a ruffled shape. Make several ruffles, then put a spot of glue on the bottom of each one and glue them on the letter.

Display the letter on the refrigerator, and have the child identify it each time he or she opens the refrigerator door. Make additional lacy letters to add to the collection.

BEAN BAGS

Turn those old worn-out jeans into something new.

WHAT YOU'LL NEED: Old jeans, marker, scissors, needle and thread, beans, three or more shoe boxes, paper

Not only are bean bags an ideal project for recycling old jeans, but what better way for the child to learn about the letter *B* sound than with "beans" and "bags?"

Put the jeans on a flat surface, and trace two 4" × 4" squares on top of a pant leg with a marker. Cut out the squares. (Since jean material is heavy, an adult should cut the material.) After the squares have been cut out, ask the child to put the squares together like a sandwich, with the finished sides touching. Stitch around three sides of the squares, creating a pocket with a ¼" seam, then turn the pocket inside out. (The seam will be inside the pocket, and the finished side will be showing.)

As the child puts beans into the pocket, or "bag," he or she can count them. Fill the bag about three-fourths full, emphasizing the word *bean* several times, then turn in the top edges of the open side and sew them together. Ask the child to tell you what was made, the steps taken to make the bean bag, and the *B* words used *(bean, bag)*.

Assign a letter to each shoe box. A simple way to do this is to place a small piece of paper on which the chosen letter has been written inside each box. Place the boxes next to or near each other several yards away, and see if the child can toss the bean bag into one of the containers. Finally, name a word (or several words) that begin with that letter.

LEFT OR RIGHT

Use your hands and letter sounds to learn the difference between left and right.

WHAT YOU'LL NEED: Red and blue tempera paint, paintbrush, white paper

A prerequisite for reading is to be able to differentiate between left and right, since the reading process requires a left-to-right progression. The concepts of left and right can be confusing for a child, but with a little help from painted hands, a memory association can be made.

Use a paintbrush to paint the palm of the child's right hand red. Emphasize the beginning sound of *right* and *red*. Then make an impression of that painted hand on a piece of white paper. Next, use blue paint to make a similar impression using the child's left palm. After the child's hands are washed and the hand prints are dry, he or she can practice matching both hands to the prints. To further assist the child, a red ribbon may be tied around the right wrist, a blue ribbon around the left one.

RIDDLE TIME

I shout out "cock-a-doodle-do."
That is my way of saying good morning to you.
(a rooster)

WHAT'S IN A NAME?

Here's an art project that adds a new dimension to letter shapes.

WHAT YOU'LL NEED: Markers, construction paper or poster board, paints, bits of fabric, glue

Children will enjoy decorating their own and others' names with many colors and textures.

Start with the child's name. Write it in large, outlined letters on a sheet of construction paper or poster board. Brainstorm with the child to come up with different ways to decorate each letter—for example, with pictures and designs made with paint or markers, or perhaps with cut-up bits of fabric glued to the paper.

After doing his or her own name, have the child make decorative names for friends and family members. Encourage the child to personalize the decoration by using pictures, designs, and colors that remind him or her of each person.

ALPHABET ILLUSTRATION

Alphabet art lets young illustrators stretch their creative muscles.

WHAT YOU'LL NEED: Washable paints, paintbrush, paper

This activity is a great way to reinforce the idea of beginning letters.

Suggest a letter, and explain to the child that he or she should paint a picture that contains items whose names begin with the letter. For example, an *S* picture might contain a sun, sand, a sea, a sidewalk, and a sailboat. A letter *B* picture might contain a bus, building, bird, balloon, and bench. When the child completes the picture, encourage him or her to point out each item with the chosen letter.

ANIMAL FINGERS

274

Beginning sounds will be at children's fingertips in this artistic activity.

WHAT YOU'LL NEED: Felt, blunt scissors, glue or clear tape, bits of yarn, markers, construction paper

Encourage children's dramatic talents by making finger puppets that they can use to act out animal characters.

Cut out two finger-shaped pieces of felt approximately 1″ × 2″. Glue or tape them together along the edges so that the child's finger will fit into the pocket. Start with a cat character. Help the child paste on bits of yarn for whiskers and a tail, and use markers or construction paper to make eyes and ears. Have the child put the puppet on a finger and name words that begin like *cat,* using a cat's "voice." Continue by making dog, bird, lamb, and tiger puppets.

275 # ALPHABET APPLES

Get to the core of the "short" letter A.

WHAT YOU'LL NEED: Red construction paper, blunt scissors, marker or pen

Give paper apples as a reward as children learn to identify the beginning sound of the "short" letter *A.*

Cut several apples out of red construction paper. Print *Aa* on each one. Say a series of word pairs such as *car/ant.* Have the child identify the word that begins like *apple.* Other word pairs to use are *add/bear, after/cup, fire/alley, attic/uncle, peach/alligator, eat/at.* As an extra challenge, have the child draw items that begin with the "short" letter *A.*

276 — LETTER NECKLACE

Help kids make a simple necklace that they can wear with pride.

WHAT YOU'LL NEED: Index cards, marker or pen, hole puncher, 24″ length of yarn; optional: old magazines, blunt scissors, glue or clear tape, paper clip

In this activity, children can show what they've learned by wearing it around their necks.

Use six to eight index cards. On the first card, write a letter. On each of the other cards, the child should make a picture of an item whose name begins with that letter. Or you can ask the child to cut out magazine pictures of objects that have the same first letter and glue or tape them on the cards.

When the child has completed the cards, punch two holes at the top of each one. String the yarn through the cards, keeping the letter card in the center. Have the child name the letter and the pictured items. Put the stringed cards around the child's neck so he or she can wear them like a necklace. Fasten the ends fairly loosely with a paper clip (to prevent a choking hazard).

RIDDLE TIME

Why shouldn't you tell a cow a secret?
Because cattle tattle.

277 DIP AND DYE

▼▼▼▼▼▼▼▼▼▼▼▼▼▼▼▼▼▼▼▼▼▼▼▼▼▼▼▼▼▼▼

*See what happens when you dip coffee filters
into colored water.*

WHAT YOU'LL NEED: Small containers, food coloring, coffee filters, old newspapers

Dipped and dyed coffee filters look beautiful and are an easy way for a child to learn some new *D* words.

Pour some water into small containers. Fill them about half full. Have the child add a different food coloring to each container. Discuss with the child the colors that were added and their beginning letter sounds—for example, *R* for red, *B* for blue, *G* for green, and so on.

Have the child fold a coffee filter into small sections. Ask him or her to think of a *D* word to describe a way to get the colored water on the folded coffee filter. Then have the child dip part of the filter into one of the colored water containers. Repeat dipping into the other colors using different parts of the filter. When the child has finished dipping the filter, open it up and place it on newspapers to dry.

Ask the child the following questions. "What *D* word did you do to the filter?" (Answer: *dip.*) "What happened to the white filter when it was dipped into colored water?" (Answer: It was dyed.) Have the child describe what colors he or she sees on the filter, and what happened when some colors were mixed together. Ask him or her to name the beginning letters of those colors.

LETTER HEADBAND

278

Stylish kids will enjoy making wearable art with letters.

WHAT YOU'LL NEED: Construction paper, blunt scissors, glue or clear tape, stapler, pen or pencil, crayons or colored markers

In this activity, the alphabet goes to children's heads!

Cut a long strip of construction paper about 3″ wide. Put the strip around the child's head. Find a comfortable fit for the headband, and staple the ends of the band together.

On sheets of construction paper, draw outlines of letters and have the child color them in. Discuss the names of the letters as he or she colors. You may want to focus on one letter or on several letters. Cut out the letters, and help the child glue or tape them onto the headband. The child can wear the headband, or take it off and name the letters.

279

GET IN SHAPE

Cookie cutters can be fun even if you aren't doing any baking.

WHAT YOU'LL NEED: Cookie cutters shaped like various objects, paper, pen or pencil, crayons or colored markers, blunt scissors

Children will enjoy using cookie cutter shapes to work on beginning sounds.

Find cookie cutters of various recognizable shapes, such as a tree, a bell, or a specific animal. Trace each shape on a sheet of paper, then ask the child to color and decorate each shape. Next, have the child name each shape and the letter that begins its name. Write this letter on each shape, then cut them all out. Have the child pick a shape, name the letter on it, and say a word that begins with the same letter.

ICE CUBE PAINTING

Run out of tempera paint? Try painting with colored ice cubes.

WHAT YOU'LL NEED: Styrofoam egg carton, food coloring, Popsicle sticks, paintbrush, white paper, pen or marker

You will need to make colored ice cubes before doing this activity. Use an empty Styrofoam egg carton, filling each section three-fourths of the way with water.

Have the child squeeze drops of different food colors into the various sections of the egg carton. As the child is squeezing a particular color, ask him or her to name the color and then tell you what letter and letter sound is heard at the beginning of that color word—for example, *R* for red, *Y* for yellow, and so on. Encourage the child to mix some of the food colors to make new colors (blue and red make purple; yellow and red make orange). Place the egg carton in the freezer. When the colored water is nearly frozen, add Popsicle sticks to serve as handles for painting.

Give the child a paintbrush and instruct him or her to brush water over a sheet of white paper while you are breaking the Styrofoam egg carton to remove the frozen colored ice cubes. Ask the child to select a colored ice cube, and have him or her tell you the beginning letter sound of that cube's color. Have the child hold the cube by the Popsicle stick handle and "paint" on the wet piece of paper. Different letters and designs can be created. When these paintings are dry, you and the child can title them.

281 ·········· ROCK PERSON ··········

Make a rock character, and roll with the letter R.

WHAT YOU'LL NEED: Rock, yarn, glue, blunt scissors, marker or pen, construction paper, clear tape

Reinforce the letter *R* with a "person" made from a rock.

Help the child find a smooth, medium-sized rock. Cut lengths of yarn and have the child glue them to the top of the rock to serve as hair. Have the child draw arms, legs, and facial features on construction paper. Cut them out, and glue or tape them to the rock. Ask the child to say additional words that begin with the letter *R*.

PEEK-A-BOO WINDOWS 282

Open windows of opportunity to practice beginning sounds.

WHAT YOU'LL NEED: Construction paper, blunt scissors, drawing paper, marker or pen

In this activity, children create windows that they can open to identify the pictures inside and make their beginning sounds.

Fold a sheet of construction paper in half, from top to bottom. On one half, draw two large squares. Cut three sides of each square and fold the paper back to form a flap. Fold a sheet of drawing paper in half, also from top to bottom. Make a "book" by folding the construction paper, flap side on top, over the drawing paper.

Mark the positions of the construction paper squares on the paper. Ask the child to draw a picture of an object in each square on the drawing paper. Put the construction paper cover back on the paper. Ask the child to open each flap and identify the object in each window, along with the object's beginning sound. Continue by creating new pages of pictures to put inside the construction paper cover.

SOUND STAGE

283

Set the stage for fun by designing a diorama.

WHAT YOU'LL NEED: Shoe box, construction paper, crayons, found objects

Challenge a child's creativity by making a three-dimensional diorama that illustrates a beginning sound.

First, discuss with the child a possible theme for a diorama based on a single beginning sound—such as "Patsy Petunia's Palace," "Timmy Turtle's Tree," or "Sandy's Sports Store."

Turn the shoe box on its side, and show the child how to decorate the floor, ceiling, and walls of the diorama with crayons and construction paper. Then have the child make or collect objects for the diorama that start with the same beginning sound. For example, "Patsy Petunia's Palace" could contain Patsy, a petunia, a pig, a picture, and pots and pans. Use your imagination!

284

TV STAR

Acting out a favorite nursery rhyme is even more fun "on-screen."

WHAT YOU'LL NEED: Large cardboard box, knife, crayons

Reinforce children's enjoyment of rhyme as they "star" on their own television screen.

Find a very large box such as one used for a large appliance. Cut a large square hole in one side of the box (keep the knife out of the reach of the child). Have the child decorate the "television" with knobs and controls. Then have the child recite and act out a nursery rhyme on the TV screen—that is, from inside the box.

The child may choose to be a character from such rhymes as "Mary, Mary, Quite Contrary," "Little Jack Horner," "Mary Had a Little Lamb," or "Jack and Jill."

285 ...... SHAPE WIND CHIMES

Hear lovely sounds when the wind blows these "chimes."

WHAT YOU'LL NEED: Clay, wax paper, rolling pin, plastic knife, pencil, string, 6" dowel rod or stick

Small hand muscles will be used as the child kneads and squeezes clay to make it pliable.

Give the child a ball of clay to knead and soften. As he or she is squeezing and "working" the clay (on a piece of wax paper), ask him or her, "How does it feel, and what shape does it have?" Look around the room and find other shapes—for example, a rectangle, square, triangle, and diamond. Talk about them and identify their beginning letter sounds (the letter *R* for rectangle, *S* for square, and so on).

When the clay is softened, have the child roll it with a rolling pin to make it flat. Help him or her cut out shapes from the clay with a plastic knife. Give directions as follows: "Make a shape that begins with an *R*." Continue with the other beginning letters *(S, T, D)* to create different shapes.

Carefully lift the clay shapes, and put them on another sheet of wax paper. Take a pencil and make a hole at the top of each shape. When the clay is thoroughly dry, ask the child to help you tie one end of string to each shape (through each hole) and the other end of the string to a stick or dowel rod. Tie another piece of string to the rod so the shapes can be hung as wind "chimes."

As you and the child are hanging these chimes where the wind can blow them, ask him or her to name the *W* word that causes the chimes to make sounds. (Answer: *wind*.) Review the beginning sounds of the suspended shapes.

286 FUN FOLDERS

Make a collage of items that begin with the letter F.

WHAT YOU'LL NEED: File folders, marker or pen, old magazines, blunt scissors, glue or clear tape

A file folder makes an excellent organizer for pictures illustrating beginning sounds.

Print the letters *Ff* on the front of a folder. Have the child look through magazines for pictures of objects whose names begin with the letter *F*. Cut out the pictures and arrange them in an interesting layout across the middle of the opened folder. Glue or tape the pictures in place. You can make additional folders for other letters of the alphabet.

POTATO PRINT LETTERS 287

You can bake them, cook them, mash them, and fry them.
You can also paint with them.

WHAT YOU'LL NEED: Potato, knife, letter stencils, marker, tempera paint, paper, clean Styrofoam meat tray

In this activity, the child will stamp letters using potatoes.

Cut a potato in half. Using a letter stencil and marker, trace a letter onto the cut surface of the potato. Use a knife to shave down the potato around the letter. The letter will then be raised, allowing it to be printed.

Hint: Unless the letter you choose is symmetrical (such as capital letters *A, H, I, M, O, T, V, W, X,* and *Y*), it will need to be stenciled backwards so that the letter print will not be reversed. Pour some paint into the meat tray. Have the child take the potato, dip it into the paint so that the raised letter is covered, and then make several letter prints on a sheet of paper. Additional letters may be cut for different letter prints.

LETTERS EVERYWHERE 288

Making a collage of letters is a wonderful way to learn the alphabet.

WHAT YOU'LL NEED: Old magazines, blunt scissors, 9″ × 12″ white construction paper, glue

As a child reads, many different sizes and types of print will need to be recognized. This activity will call attention to the variety of fonts and print sizes.

Give the child old magazines. The challenge will be to locate and then cut out large, single letters, both capital and lowercase, from advertisements. After many letters are cut, have the child paste them on a piece of white construction paper in a collage format, covering the paper and overlapping the letters. Have the child read you the letters.

289 VERY SPECIAL VEST

Turn a brown paper bag into a beautiful vest with a few simple cuts and some decorations.

WHAT YOU'LL NEED: Brown paper bag, crayons, blunt scissors, materials beginning with the letter *V* (such as velvet and Velcro), glue

To stimulate the child's creativity and to encourage the learning of *V* words, help the child make a vest to wear.

Take a brown grocery bag and turn it inside out. On one of the long sides, in the middle, make a cut from the bag's open end to the bottom of the bag at the opposite end, where you'll next cut out a hole for the child's head and neck. Hold the bag next to the child to get the correct placement for the two arm holes along the sides of the bag. Mark and cut out the arm holes. Use velvet, violet-colored materials, or anything else you can think of that begins with the letter *V* to decorate the vest.

CLAY POTTERY

A handmade piece of coiled pottery will be perfect for your table.

WHAT YOU'LL NEED: Clay, wax paper, small container of water

A child's hands will get a lot of exercise as clay is softened and then rolled into coils to form a piece of pottery.

Have the child "work" a ball of clay by kneading it to soften it. When the clay is soft, tell the child to pull off some clay from the ball and press that piece flat with his or her hand into a circle shape. It's best to do this on a sheet of wax paper. Tell the child, "I am thinking of a word that begins with the same sound as the word *red*. This word describes what you can do to the rest of the clay to make long thin strips. What word is it?" (Answer: *roll*.) As the child is rolling the clay, ask, "What other *R* words can you think of?" (*Rub* and *round* are two possibilities.)

When the clay has been shaped into several rolls (coils), have the child take one and wrap it around the edge of the clay circle. Continue placing the other coils on top of the previous ones. When all the coils are on the base, forming a pot, ask the child to gently rub the inside of the coiled rolls to smooth and seam them together. If the clay is too dry, the child can dip his or her finger into some water and then smooth the inside of the pot.

Discuss with the child what *R* words were used in making this coiled pot. After a few days of drying and hardening, the pot is ready for a special spot in your home.

SPONGE PAINTING

291

Speckled sponge patterns can make letter shapes special.

WHAT YOU'LL NEED: Small sponges, paint, paper

Children will enjoy the patterns created by using a sponge as a painting tool.

To make the sponges, you can cut a new kitchen sponge into pieces approximately 1″ × 2″. Put tempera paint, finger paint, or poster paint in a shallow dish. Show the child how to dip a sponge in the paint and stamp it on a sheet of paper. (Heavy art paper will work best, but any kind of paper will do.)

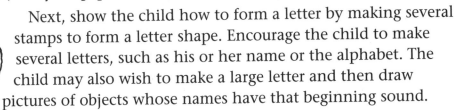

Next, show the child how to form a letter by making several stamps to form a letter shape. Encourage the child to make several letters, such as his or her name or the alphabet. The child may also wish to make a large letter and then draw pictures of objects whose names have that beginning sound.

292

BUILDING BOXES

Building with boxes can build a child's ability to identify letters.

WHAT YOU'LL NEED: Boxes of various sizes and shapes

Begin this activity by asking the child to think of different things that might be found in a box. Then see how many different boxes can be located in the home.

After several boxes are collected, ask the child to build something using these boxes as building blocks. Whatever the child constructs—a castle, tunnel, tower, house, or something else—ask him or her to identify the beginning letter of that structure. Ask the child what else he or she can build with the boxes.

QUILT MAKING

293

Keep warm by wrapping yourself up in a beautiful quilt.

WHAT YOU'LL NEED: Sixteen 10″ × 10″ pieces of loosely woven fabric (for example, burlap), plastic needle, thread

The letter Q is a difficult letter for a child to identify and learn because there are so few Q words. Tell the child that Q is so quiet that it needs a *u* standing next to it to make words.

Help the child make a quilt. Cut out 16 pieces of material measuring 10″ × 10″. The child can then take the squares and arrange them on the floor in four rows of four.

Using a plastic threaded needle, sew the squares with a simple up-and-down stitch. Keep adding squares. It is best to sew four squares together into a panel and then sew the panels together. Talk with the child about a quilt—how it may be used, why people make quilts, and the beginning letters and letter sounds in the word *quilt*.

294

FUNNY FOAM

Letters written in shaving cream will leave an impression on youngsters.

WHAT YOU'LL NEED: Shaving cream, waxed paper, paper, marker or pen

Encourage children to learn letter formation as they have fun putting their hands in shaving cream.

Spread a layer of shaving cream on a sheet of waxed paper. Write a letter on a sheet of paper, and have the child copy the letter by "writing" it with a finger in the shaving cream. Show the child how to "erase" the letter by smoothing over the cream. Continue writing letters for the child to copy, or say words and see if the child can write the letters representing the beginning sounds.

CLAY PLAY DAY

Every child is a sculptor in this easy letter-formation activity.

WHAT YOU'LL NEED: Clay or homemade modeling dough (see recipe below), paper, marker or pen

Forming three-dimensional letters allows children to experience the alphabet with their sense of touch as well as sight.

To make claylike dough at home, heat a mixture of 1½ cups of water and ½ cup of salt until it is almost boiling. Remove the mixture from the heat. Add two tablespoons of salad oil and two tablespoons powdered alum (available in the spice aisle in the supermarket). Cool the mixture for five minutes. Work in two to three cups of flour with your hands. The dough can be stored in plastic bags at room temperature and can be used for about a month.

Show the child how to roll small balls of clay into coils about six inches long. Or you may choose to cut strips from a flat sheet of clay. Write a letter on a sheet of paper. Have the child form the letter with clay strips. Start with simple letters, such as *T* and *L*, and continue with more complex letters such as *A* and *B*.

NURSERY RHYME

Sammy the snake is sleeping,
when suddenly he awakes.
S-s-s
is the soft little sound he makes.

Sammy the snake is crawling,
over the leaves on the ground.
S-s-s
Sammy makes a soft little sound.

296 MARBLE ROLLS

Beautiful designs can be made by rolling marbles in paint.

WHAT YOU'LL NEED: Aluminum pie pan, paper to fit bottom of pan, tempera paint, marble, clothespin, container for small amount of paint

With this activity, the child will be developing fine motor skills—both by using a clothespin to pick up the marble and by tilting the pan to make the marble to move.

Pose a riddle to the child and have him or her guess what the answer is. Say, "I am thinking of something round that begins with an *M* sound, can be rolled, and sometimes is used in playing games. What is it?" After the child responds that the object is a marble, tell him or her that marbles can also be used in art. Follow these simple steps.

1. Put a piece of paper, sized to fit, in the bottom of an aluminum pan.

2. Pour enough paint into a small container so that a marble could be completely submerged in it.

3. Have the child put the marble in the paint.

4. Using a clothespin, the child picks up the marble from the paint and drops it onto the paper in the pan.

5. Tilt the pan from side to side, causing the marble to roll in different directions.

6. Remove the marble from the pan.

7. When the painting is dry, remove it from the pan. A design will be printed on the paper.

Note: For a younger child, use a box and an old tennis ball (since marbles can be a choking hazard). Emphasize the sound of the letter *T*.

297 PICTURE PLATES

Present children with a full plate of beginning sounds.

WHAT YOU'LL NEED: Small paper plates, old magazines, blunt scissors, glue or clear tape

In this activity, children use paper picture plates to work on beginning sounds.

First, help the child look through old magazines and find five or six pictures of objects, each of which is a different color (a red car, a green field, a blue pen, a black building, an orange vegetable, and so on). Cut out the pictures, and glue or tape each one onto a paper plate. Stack the plates. Ask the child, "Can you find a picture of something green?" Have the child find the green picture, identify the object, and say a word that has the same beginning sound. Continue through the entire stack of plates.

HANDY GIFT WRAP 298

Here's an easy way to personalize your gift-wrapping paper.

WHAT YOU'LL NEED: Large sheet of thin or regular paper, tempera paint, paintbrush

Relatives and friends will love this special handprint wrapping paper.

Lay out a large sheet of thin or regular paper and several bottles of tempera paint. Let the child select the colors of paint that he or she wants to use. Ask him or her to tell you the beginning letters of the colors selected—for example, *R* for red, *P* for purple.

Ask the child to name the part of the body that begins with an *H* and which can be used to make prints with paint. (Answer: hand.) Next, take the colors of paints the child selected and brush paint on the child's palm with a paintbrush. While doing this, reinforce the *H* sound of the word *hand*. When the child's hand is painted, have him or her press the hand all over the paper to make colored prints.

299 — — — SUN SHAPES — — —

Next time there's a sunny day, try making these
sun-bleached prints.

WHAT YOU'LL NEED: Collection of familiar objects (such as a pencil,
ruler, marker, and paper clip), dark-colored construction
paper, marker or pen

This activity blends science and phonics.

On a sunny day, help the child collect
some objects that are easily
recognizable by their shapes—for
example, a pencil, ruler, marker, and paper
clip. Discuss the beginning letters and sounds of those
objects.

Next, ask the child to select a piece of dark-colored construction paper. Then take the
collected objects and the paper outside. Place the paper on the ground, in direct sunlight,
and have the child arrange the objects on the paper. (You may need to place some heavy
stones on the edges of the paper if it is a windy day.)

Approximately one hour later, instruct the child to remove the objects from the paper.
Ask the child what he or she sees, and discuss what happened to the paper. As each image is
identified, have him or her use a marker or pen to write the beginning letter under each
image left under the object (*P* for pencil, *M* for marker, *R* for ruler, and so on).

LID O's

▼▼▼▼▼▼▼▼▼▼▼▼▼▼▼▼▼▼▼▼▼▼▼▼▼▼▼▼▼▼

*What letter can you print with a lid? Dip one in
paint and find out.*

WHAT YOU'LL NEED: Collection of lids of various sizes, tempera
paint, small containers, sheet of paper

The child will learn all about *O*'s in this colorful activity.

Ask the child to help you find and collect lids of various
sizes, then pour some paint into several small containers. Have
the child guess what letter will be made when the lid is pressed on the
paper. (Answer: *O*.)

Next, select a lid and dip its edge into the paint. Press the lid onto the paper. As the child
prints the letter on a sheet of paper, ask him or her what letter is being made. Make several
prints with that lid, then have the child select another lid that will make a bigger or smaller
letter *O* and make prints with those. When the prints are dry, ask the child which letter *O*'s
are capital letters and which ones are lowercase letters—and why.

GOOEY GLOP

■ ■ ■ ■ ■ ■ ■ ■ ■ ■ ■ ■ ■ ■ ■

*Half the fun of this letter activity is mixing up
the gooey dough.*

WHAT YOU'LL NEED: Ingredients for Gooey Glop (see below), plastic bag

Children can make three-dimensional letters with this homemade modeling dough.

Mix two cups of salt and ⅔ cup of water. Heat until almost boiling. In a separate bowl,
mix one cup of cornstarch and ½ cup of cold water. Pour it into the hot salt-and-water
mixture. Let it cool.

Say words, and have the child use the Gooey Glop to shape letters that stand for the
beginning sounds. The child can work with the dough on a kitchen counter or a plastic
surface. Store the dough in a plastic bag and reuse it.

CHAIN OF LETTERS

302

This activity helps mend missing links in alphabet identification.

WHAT YOU'LL NEED: Construction paper, blunt scissors, glue or clear tape, marker or pen

Gluing strips of paper to make a chain is a great exercise for hand-eye coordination.

Cut 26 strips of paper measuring approximately 6″ in length. Write both the capital and lowercase forms of a letter on each one: *Aa, Bb,* and so on through the alphabet. Help the child make a paper chain by gluing or taping the first strip of paper into a circle. Continue to glue the strips into circles, one linked with the next, to make a chain. When the chain is finished, ask the child to name the letter on each link.

303

SURF'S UP!

A smart whale can help alphabet surfers challenge the waves.

WHAT YOU'LL NEED: Large sheet of art paper, crayons or colored markers (including blue), piece of gray poster board, blunt scissors, glue or clear tape, Popsicle stick

Here's a whale of a game that makes identifying letters fun.

On a large sheet of paper, draw ocean waves. Make at least 10 wave peaks. At the top of each wave peak, write a letter. Have the child color the ocean blue. Next, ask the child to draw the outline of a whale on a piece of gray poster board. Cut it out, and glue or tape the whale to a Popsicle stick.

To play the game, ask the child to make the whale travel over the waves. In order to go from one wave to the next, the child must identify the letter on the wave. If the child misses a letter, he or she must go back to the beginning.

304 ● VEGETABLE PRINTS

What better way to learn about vegetables than to make art prints with them.

WHAT YOU'LL NEED: Tempera paint, several clean Styrofoam meat trays, vegetables (such as pepper, mushroom, broccoli, cauliflower, radish, carrot, onion, potato), construction paper, marker

Vegetables such as peppers and onions have distinctive aromas. In addition, they have distinctive shapes and textures.

Pour some tempera paint onto several Styrofoam meat trays. Show the child some vegetables, and see if he or she can identify them. Then ask, "What letter does the word *vegetables* begin with?" Cut portions of the vegetables so that the child can handle them.

Have the child select a cut vegetable, then tell you what it is and its beginning letter. Next, instruct the child to dip the cut vegetable into the paint and "print" it on the paper. Continue with different vegetables and paints.

When the prints are dry, ask the child, "What type of food beginning with the letter *V* was used to make all the prints?" Discuss the shapes and characteristics of each vegetable as the child points to its print and says its beginning letter. Have the child write that letter under each vegetable print with a marker.

305 MONEY ART

Here's an interesting way to "make" some money.

WHAT YOU'LL NEED: Penny, nickel, dime, quarter, crayons, thin or regular paper

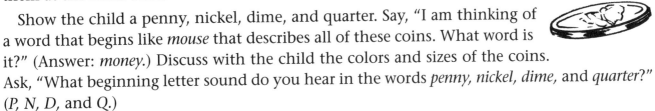

The child will be using small hand muscles as he or she is making rubbings of different coins and learning about them at the same time.

Show the child a penny, nickel, dime, and quarter. Say, "I am thinking of a word that begins like *mouse* that describes all of these coins. What word is it?" (Answer: *money.*) Discuss with the child the colors and sizes of the coins. Ask, "What beginning letter sound do you hear in the words *penny, nickel, dime,* and *quarter*?" (*P, N, D,* and *Q.*)

Have the child select a crayon and a coin. Put a sheet of thin or regular paper over the coin, and instruct the child to rub the crayon over the paper where the coin is. This will create an imprint of the coin. Repeat this with the other coins. When all of the money has been rubbed, have the child match the coins to the coin imprints and write the beginning letter of each coin next to the corresponding crayon imprint.

RIDDLE TIME

Who am I?
I say "moo" and nibble on grass and hay.
I give the farmer milk every day.

(a cow)

306 LETTER SELF-PORTRAIT

Help a child make a revealing life-size self-portrait.

WHAT YOU'LL NEED: Large sheet of heavy kraft paper, crayons or markers

Do this project to personalize a child's study of letters.

Find a large sheet of paper that is sturdy and a few inches longer than the child's height. Put the paper on the floor, have the child lie on it, and trace around him or her. Have the child color the "self-portrait" with crayons or markers and print his or her name at the top.

Encourage the child to add distinguishing characteristics of dress, hairstyle, and so on. Write the first letter of the child's name, and have the child draw pictures of toys whose names begin with that letter.

WORD BALLOONS 307

Put letters together and celebrate with colorful balloons.

WHAT YOU'LL NEED: Construction paper, blunt scissors, marker or pen, index cards

In this activity, children can learn how to put letters together to make words using balloon shapes.

Cut a balloon shape out of construction paper, and write the word ending *an* on it. Print the lowercase letters *c, f, t, m, p,* and *r* on index cards. Have the child put each letter card in front of the word ending on the balloon and say the new word. You can make other word balloons using the word endings *at, ell, op,* and *ot.* (Point out that not all letter combinations will form words.)

308 WALL HANGING

A burlap wall hanging is just what you need for that empty wall.

WHAT YOU'LL NEED: 18" × 24" piece of burlap, old ribbon and/or thick yarn

By going over and under burlap threads with some yarn, you can make a beautiful wall hanging—and learn a few letters as well.

With the finished edges of the burlap at the top and bottom, prepare the piece of burlap by removing cross threads from along the unfinished edges. This will leave open spaces in the material for the child to weave in different materials.

Show the child the piece of burlap with the open spaces and the yarn, and then say, "I am thinking of two words, one beginning with an *O* and the other with a *U,* that you can use to help you fill the open areas of the burlap. How can you put some yarn in those places?" (Answer: *over* and *under*.) Have the child select some yarn, and try going "over" and "under" the lengthwise threads. Explain that this process, going over and under, is called weaving.

Ask the child, "What letter does the word *weaving* begin with?" As the child is weaving, have him or her say "over" and "under" during the weaving process. Even if a few threads are skipped, the effect will still be beautiful. Try different thicknesses and colors of yarn and/or ribbon for a distinctive weaving.

TWIST IT

309

Use pipe cleaners to demonstrate the twists and turns of beginning sounds.

WHAT YOU'LL NEED: Pipe cleaners

It's easy to create all kinds of objects by twisting pipe cleaners. This activity encourages children to think of the beginning sounds in the names of the objects they make.

Show the child how to twist pipe cleaners into the shape of an apple, a car, or a stick person. After the child has made several items, have him or her group them according to beginning sounds. On other occasions, make a group of objects whose names have specific beginning sounds.

310

LETTER MOBILE

Collect two- and three-dimensional items for this mobile display.

WHAT YOU'LL NEED: Construction paper, pen or marker, blunt scissors, hole puncher, string or yarn, wire coat hanger, old magazines, collected items (see below)

A mobile is an interesting way to display a letter. Have the child choose a letter. Draw it on construction paper, and cut it out. Punch a small hole in the top, attach a piece of yarn or string, and hang it from the hanger.

Have the child collect pictures and other items whose names begin with the same letter. For example, choosing the letter *C*, the child might find a paper cup, a cookie cutter, and a picture of a cat. Hang the items on the mobile with string or yarn of varying lengths.

ALPHABET ADVENTURES

Is it possible for children who never stop moving to learn letter sounds and word recognition? For parents and teachers who have wondered about this, Chapter 7 offers activities with the emphasis on *active*. Sports lovers can play "Phonetic Football," "Beginning Sound Baseball," and "Basketball Fun." You will also find activities to play on a bus or in a car. To fend off the dreaded question, "Are we there yet?", try "Travel Tall Tales" and "Alphabet Categories."

311 — CLIMB EVERY MOUNTAIN

See who's king of the mountain when it comes to beginning sounds.

WHAT YOU'LL NEED: Index cards, marker or pen, blankets

Give active children a goal to reach as they practice beginning sounds.

First, make letter cards by printing letters on index cards. Make a "mountain" by stacking blankets in a big mound on the floor. You may put cushions and pillows in the center of the mound to support the mountain. Put letter cards in folds of the blankets all the way up and around the mountain. Challenge the child to climb the mountain by identifying each letter on the way to the top and saying a word in which that letter stands for the beginning sound.

As children become better at identifying the letters and sounds, have them start over at the bottom if they give an incorrect answer. If you have a real hill or something else that can be climbed in your backyard, try this activity outside.

312 DOCTOR'S VISIT

Turn a routine doctor's visit into a learning experience by looking at X rays.

WHAT YOU'LL NEED: Alphabet cards, dictionary

Here's an activity that will help the child learn about the rarely used letter *X*.

On a routine doctor or dentist visit, ask the doctor or dentist (or an assistant) to show the child an X ray and discuss its creation and function. If time permits, let the child see an X ray machine and how it works. This may help alleviate any fears the child may have about getting an X ray taken.

At home, show the letter *X* to the child, be it on an alphabet card or in the dictionary.

313 O, O, OPPOSITE

Up and down, in and out. Here's a game of opposites.

Short vowel sounds are challenging for a child to learn, but if he or she can remember a key word, the task becomes easier. To help a child learn the short *O* sound, play "O, O, Opposite."

In this game, you say one word or do some action, and the child responds with the opposite word or action. For example, you sit down, and the child stands up. You walk forward, and the child walks backward. You point to something black, and the child points to something white. You touch the top of something, and the child touches the bottom. Continually point out that the child is doing the *opposite*. This game also involves the concept of directional words.

HAMBURGER HARRY

314

Favorite foods come to life—and teach the sound of the letter H.

WHAT YOU'LL NEED: Paper hamburger box, markers, construction paper, glue or clear tape

Creating a hamburger-box person makes learning the *H* sound fun.

Help the child use markers and pieces of construction paper to make facial features on the top of the hamburger box. Show the child how to open and close the hamburger's "mouth" by opening and shutting the box. Then have the child use the hamburger person's voice to tell an *H*-word story. For example: "A *hamburger hopped* to a *house* to *help* a *hungry hippopotamus*."

315

NUTS AND BOLTS

In addition to nuts and bolts, what else can you find at a hardware store?

On your next trip to the hardware store, have the child accompany you and discover the letters and letter sounds of the materials found there.

As you and the child stroll down the aisles of the store, stop and say, "I see something beginning with the letter *P*. What could it be?" (Answer: paint.) See how many different beginning letters you can find and name. Some items to look for are: bolts, file, hammer, ladder, mailbox, nuts, rope, sandpaper, tacks, and wallpaper.

On your way home, talk about the many items that you saw at the hardware store and the different beginning-letter sounds of those things.

OUTDOOR ART WALK

316

Find everything from A to Z when you go outdoors and look carefully.

WHAT YOU'LL NEED: Notepad, pencil

This activity takes the child outside of the home to find things that begin with different letters of the alphabet. Besides expanding the scope of the child's environment, it reinforces the idea that objects outside the home also have beginning sounds.

Bring a notepad on which you have written the alphabet, one letter per line, down the left side. Use as many pages as you need to complete the alphabet. As a certain object is identified by the child, have him or her tell you what the first letter of the word is. For example: acorn = *A*; bird = *B*; vine = *V*; tree = *T*. Write the object's name next to the corresponding letter on the notepad.

Note: If you can't find an *X* but still want to make use of the letter, put an *X* over every letter for which you find an object.

317

NAME THAT CARD

Playing cards aren't just for playing. They can be used to teach beginning sounds.

WHAT YOU'LL NEED: Deck of playing cards

In this game, children can learn the basics of playing card games as they work on beginning sounds.

Shuffle the cards. Show the child one card at a time, and say its number or name (jack, queen, king, ace). Have the child say a word that has the same beginning sound. If the answer is correct, give the child the card. Continue until the child has won several cards. As the child learns the names of the cards, he or she can say the name of each card, as well as a word with the same beginning sound.

318 LIBRARY VISIT

▼▼▼▼▼▼▼▼▼▼▼▼▼▼▼▼▼▼▼▼▼▼▼▼▼▼▼▼▼▼▼▼▼

A trip to the library is a perfect activity for a rainy day.

Have an enriching experience by taking the child to visit a library. This activity exposes the child to the concept of alphabetical order and the purpose and use of a library. It will also help him or her develop an appreciation for books by showing how they are an invaluable source of information.

Give the child a topic such as animals. Ask him or her to name an animal that begins with the letter *H.* If the child says *horse,* look for an easy informational book about that animal, such as an encyclopedia or encyclopedic dictionary.

Use the library's computerized card catalog (if possible) to identify specific book titles, then show the child how to find the books on the shelves. Select several books and check them out. Read the books to the child, and have him or her answer the questions that were asked.

NURSERY RHYME

Buzzy is a little fly
who lives not far away.
He wakes me every morning
at the break of day.
z-z-z

He wakes me quite early
by nibbling on my toes.
z-z-z
Then he teases Daddy
by buzzing on his nose.
z-z-z

BEAN BAG TOSS

Ready, set, toss. Where did that bean bag land?

WHAT YOU'LL NEED: Old shower curtain or plastic tablecloth, bean bag, marker

This is a good activity for an energetic child.

Find an old shower curtain or tablecloth. On an unprinted side, write the letters of the alphabet in scrambled order. Make the letters fairly large, but try to spread them out so that the they are at least a few inches apart and cover most of the surface. Place this alphabet sheet on the floor. Give the child a bean bag (see "Bean Bags" on page 174 for directions on how to make one), and ask him or her to toss it onto the sheet from several feet away. Have the child say the name of the letter closest to the spot where the bean bag lands.

Variation: Call out a letter first, and then tell the child to try to throw the bean bag so that it lands on that letter. Or, instead of saying a letter, say a word, then have the child identify the beginning letter and try to toss the bag on that letter.

RIDDLE TIME

What do you call a damp animal doctor?

A wet vet

320 PICNIC IN THE PARK

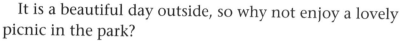

It's a perfect day for a picnic, but first you have to pack.

WHAT YOU'LL NEED: Picnic basket, foods beginning with the letter *P*

It is a beautiful day outside, so why not enjoy a lovely picnic in the park?

Have the child help you plan what to take on this picnic. However, only things that begin with the letter *P* may be taken. As you are talking, emphasize *P* words. Ask the child to think of foods that you can bring: *peanut* butter sandwiches, *peaches*, *pineapple* juice served in a *paper* cup, *potato* chips, *pretzels*. *Prepare* those foods, *pack* the *picnic* basket, and have a great time at the *park*.

OBSTACLE COURSE 321

Design your own obstacle course using a few simple materials.

WHAT YOU'LL NEED: Big boxes, hula hoop, bean bags, rope, etc.

To increase the awareness of the short *O* sound (as in the word *obstacle*) and challenge a child's motor skills at the same time, make an obstacle course.

Take large empty boxes to serve as tunnels, and arrange hula hoops, bean bags, and rope into challenging obstacles. For example, the rope can be arranged into a letter shape on which the child has to walk, tracing its formation. The hula hoop can be twirled around the waist, jumped over, hopped into, or walked around to get the *O* shape. Bean bags can be placed on a child's head as he or she is walking, testing balancing skills.

Depending on your environment and imagination, additional materials can be used to create other kinds of obstacles or challenges.

322 FEED THE BIRDS

What lovely treats for our feathered friends!

WHAT YOU'LL NEED: Pine cones, two plastic dishes, peanut butter, bird seed, plastic spoon, yarn

Find some pine cones, and as you are collecting them with the child, talk about the types of trees that have pine cones and needles. See what different sizes and types of pine cones you can find.

When you return home, tell the child that you will make a bird feeder from the pine cones. Ask, "Do you know what birds like to eat that begins like the word *sun*?" (Answer: seeds.) Put some peanut butter in one dish and bird seed in another. Have the child take a plastic spoon and spread peanut butter on a pine cone. Then have the child roll the peanut butter-covered pine cone in bird seed. The peanut butter will make the bird seed stick to the pine cone.

When several bird feeder pine cones are made, take pieces of yarn and help the child tie a knot around the top of each one. Then make a loop at the other end of the yarn, and hang the pine cones on a tree branch. As you are hanging the bird feeders, ask the child, "What two things did you use to make this that began like the word *pat*?" (Answer: pine cone and peanut butter.) "What did you put on the peanut butter-covered pine cone that begins like *sun*?" (Answer: seeds.)

Watch the tree, and see how many different birds come to eat these treats. Use a bird book to help identify them.

323 .... GROWING A YAM

Watch a yam sprout leaves and grow into a vine.

WHAT YOU'LL NEED: Yam, three toothpicks, clear glass jar, water

Buy a yam at the grocery store. In addition to learning the *Y* sound in the word *yam,* the child can experience the fun of watching the yam sprout and grow leaves.

Place three toothpicks into the yam, spaced evenly, about a quarter-inch from the top. These toothpicks will support the yam inside the jar. Have the child put the yam inside the jar so that the toothpicks rest on the jar's rim. Add enough water so that three-fourths of the yam is covered.

Have the child place the yam in a sunny location. Ask the child what he or she thinks will happen to the yam. Identify the beginning letter sound heard in the word *yam.* As the yam grows, call the child's attention to the *V* in *vine* and the *L* in *leaves.* Have the child check daily to see if more water needs to be added to the jar.

FILL IT UP! 324

Gas tank empty? Stop at the next gas station and fill both the tank and a child's mind.

Letters and letter sounds can be learned anywhere, even at a gas station. See how many different letters can be found there.

As you and the child drive into a gas station, ask him or her, "What do you see?" When the child names an object (for example, a pump), ask what beginning letter that word has. Point to other objects (tires, a hose, a windshield, a car), and talk about their beginning sounds.

On your drive home, talk about the different things the child saw and the beginning sounds of those objects.

NURSERY VISIT

Time to do some planting. Take a trip to a nursery and learn about plants.

Building one's vocabulary is a necessary part of language development. Visits to businesses offer valuable opportunities for a child to learn new words.

Visiting a garden nursery, the child learns that the word *nursery* does not always mean a place where babies or very young children are cared for. Upon arriving at a nursery, show the child the different types of plants, flowers, trees, shrubs, and other items that are available there.

Have the child select and purchase a plant to take home. Make sure the plant is suitable for a child and is nonpoisonous. On your way home, discuss what the child saw at the nursery and how to take care of the new plant. Discuss what the plant needs to grow. This can be done by saying, "I'm thinking of something that a plant needs to grow that begins with the letter *W*. What is it?" (Water.) Or: "I'm thinking of something that a plant needs to grow beginning with the letter *S*. What is it?" (Sun.)

NURSERY RHYME

Jolly Jim is a jumping jack,
a jumping jack,
a jumping jack.
Jolly Jim is a jumping jack;
he jumps up and
down with glee.

Jolly Jim pops into his box,
into his box,
into his box.
Jolly Jim pops into his box,
and says, "You can't
catch me."

326 DONKEY DE-TAILS

"Pin the Tail on the Donkey" is more than a party game when it includes letter identification.

WHAT YOU'LL NEED: Brown wrapping paper, marker or pen, blunt scissors, construction paper, clear tape, scarf for blindfold

Make a favorite children's game a learning experience.

Draw a donkey shape on a large sheet of wrapping paper, or use a ready-made game. Cut donkey tails out of construction paper, and put a piece of tape on each tail. Print a letter on each tail.

Blindfold the child and have him or her pin the tail on the donkey. If the child is playing alone, have him or her pin several tails on the donkey. Otherwise, have each child pin one tail on it. When all the tails are on the donkey, have the child (or children) identify the letter on each tail and say a word that begins with the sound the letter represents.

BLOCK PARTY 327

Kids' earliest toys can become three-dimensional learning tools.

WHAT YOU'LL NEED: Set of building blocks with letters, paper, marker or pen

Here's an activity that makes children's play with building blocks even more instructive.

Print a word on a sheet of paper. Have the child find the blocks with the letters that spell the word and arrange them in order. Words to start with are *cat, dog, boy, top, big, fan, run, jump, play, ball,* and *girl*. As the child progresses, you might spell words with a theme, such as animal words or family words. You might also have the child spell the words.

BEGINNING SOUND BASEBALL

328

Even children who aren't power hitters can score a home run in this game.

WHAT YOU'LL NEED: Assorted toys, four pillows or sheets of paper to serve as bases

Use this indoor or outdoor activity to teach children the fundamentals of base running in baseball and to help them practice beginning sounds.

First, set up four bases in an approximate diamond shape. At each base, put several toys whose names begin with a *B* sound—for example, a ball, a bat, a bean bag, a bear, and blocks. Mix in some toys whose names do not begin with a *B* sound—for example, a car, and a doll, and a horse. Explain to the child that, to make a home run, he or she must go to each base in order and pick up a toy whose name begins like the word *baseball.* When the child reaches home plate, he or she must name each object.

329 # CONSONANT CANS

Mix the clatter of household items with a variety of letter sounds.

WHAT YOU'LL NEED: Large coffee cans, plastic lids, marker

Children will learn beginning sounds with this grab bag activity.

First, make sure the coffee cans have no sharp edges. Print a consonant letter on the top of the can lid. Have the child look for objects whose names begin with that letter. For example, for the letter *P,* the child might find a peanut, postcard, pen, paper clip, and penny. Put the lid on the can, shake it up, and take turns removing and naming the items. Create cans with other letters.

BOX BOUNCE

330

*Here's a game that tests coordination and quickness—
both mental and physical.*

WHAT YOU'LL NEED: Small box, rubber ball

Play a ball game that will keep children active and improve their coordination while they learn letters and beginning sounds.

Show the child how to catch the ball using the box. Bounce the ball for the child to catch. If he or she catches it, the child must say a word that begins with the letter *A*. When the child catches the ball a second time, he or she must say a word beginning with *B*. Continue through the rest of the alphabet.

331

LETTER PALMS

*Here's a new way to "read palms" that children
are sure to enjoy.*

WHAT YOU'LL NEED: Newspapers, tape, blunt scissors, letter cards, paper clips

Surprise children with a "palm tree" made out of newspapers.

Roll a sheet of newspaper to the center of the sheet. Then add a second sheet so that its edge is at the center of the first sheet. Continue rolling the two sheets together, and put a piece of tape around the base to keep the tube from unraveling. Next, cut halfway down the tube you have made. Make three or four more similar cuts. Carefully pull up on the paper, and a "palm tree" will form.

Ask the child to randomly select a letter card from a stack of such cards. If the child can name a word with that beginning letter, he or she can clip the card to one of the paper palm fronds. Continue until the child has clipped several cards.

332 SWING AND SLIDE

Swings, slides, and jungle gyms! The playground is an exciting place.

A child's play environment is important for his or her muscle development. This area can also be a learning environment.

On a sunny day, take the child to the playground. As you approach the play area, ask, "What can you go back and forth on that begins like the word *sweater?*" (Answer: swing.) Next ask, "What can you go down that begins like the word *slim?*" (Answer: slide.) Give the child similar riddles for the other equipment found at the playground (a see-saw, jungle gym, sandbox, obstacle course, tunnel).

As you are going from one area of the playground to another, ask the child to think of words with different beginning-letter sounds that describe different ways to get from one place to another—for example, *jump, walk, skip, gallop, hop, run.* See if the child can think of additional words, telling you the beginning-letter sounds of each one.

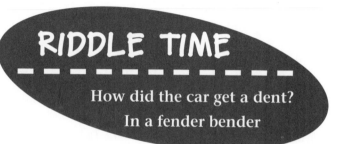

Have fun at the playground!

RIDDLE TIME

How did the car get a dent?

In a fender bender

TRAVEL TALL TALES

333

"I am going to Tallahassee, and I will take a turkey to tip the taxi driver."

This word game requires players to think of several different kinds of words beginning with a particular letter.

Using letter *A* words as an example, you can start the game by saying, "I am going to *Alabama,* and I will take *an ant* to *answer* questions." A player using letter *B* words might say, "I am going to *Boston,* and I will take a *bird* to *build* a *bungalow.*"

You can simplify the game by saying the sentence and stopping when the child must think of a word: "I am going to ____, and I will take a ____ to ____."

334 # STEPPING STONES

Practicing beginning sounds can sometimes become a balancing act.

WHAT YOU'LL NEED: Large, flat stones, letter cards

In this activity, children improve balance and dexterity as they practice beginning sounds outdoors.

In the yard or a park, find several large, flat stones and arrange them into a path. (Or you can find an existing stone path.) Make sure the child can step from one stone to the next without difficulty.

Put a different letter card on or beside each stone. Tell the child that in order to step on each stone, he or she must say a word that begins with the sound the letter stands for. If the child gives an incorrect answer, he or she must return to the beginning of the stone path.

335 SHOPPING FOR CLOTHES

Dread shopping? You won't when you try shopping this way.

Shopping for clothes with a child can be fun—and educational—when both of you know what you want.

On the way to the store, talk about different clothing items that you might find. When the child names a certain article of clothing (pants, for example), ask him or her, "What beginning letter sound do you hear?" (Answer: *P.*) Continue in the same manner for other clothing items, such as a coat, jacket, socks, and so on.

Identify the articles you want to find. When you enter the children's clothing department, knowing what needs to be purchased, ask the child to help you find the item(s). When you return home, have the child take the items you purchased out of their bags, identify the items, then tell you the beginning sound for each one.

ALPHABET RHYTHM 336

*Clap, clap, snap, snap: Follow the rhythm and
let the words flow.*

Play a rhythm game that gives children practice in quick thinking and beginning sounds.

Illustrate a rhythm pattern involving clapping hands and snapping fingers—for example: clap, clap, snap, snap. Have the child clap and snap the rhythm with you. Then tell the child that, after going through the rhythm twice, you will say a word beginning with the letter *A* sound. Then you will repeat the rhythm twice again, and he or she will say a word beginning with the *B* sound. Continue taking turns throughout the alphabet.

With advanced players, start over when a player does not think of a word in rhythm. For beginners, keep repeating the rhythm until the player thinks of a word.

BUTTON, BUTTON!

337

A misplaced button leads to a game of beginning sounds.

WHAT YOU'LL NEED: Construction paper or poster board, blunt scissors, marker or pen

Play this hiding game with a small group to give children practice with beginning sounds.

First, cut a "button" with a diameter of approximately 2" out of heavy paper or poster board. On each side of the button, write a letter. Have players sit in a circle on the floor and choose one player to be "it." The player hides his or her eyes while the other players pass the button around. After a minute or so, the player who is "it" says, "Button, button, who's got the button?" At this point, the player holding the button must hide it in his or her lap.

The player who is "it" then opens his or her eyes and tries to guess who has the button. If the guess is correct, the child who is "it" must identify the letter on top of the button and say a word in which that letter is the beginning sound. If he or she is correct, then the person hiding the button becomes "it."

338

VANILLA OR CHOCOLATE?

What flavor cone would you like?

Take some time out on a hot summer day, and visit an ice cream shop with the child.

On your way to the shop, ask the child, "What flavors of ice cream do you think the shop will have?" Upon entering the store, look together at the different pictures and advertisements for ice cream treats and the listings of ice cream flavors. Say, "I see a flavor beginning with a *V*. What do you think it could be?" (Answer: vanilla.) Repeat with other flavors.

LETTER DROP

339

A handkerchief and a group of friends add fun to this learning activity.

WHAT YOU'LL NEED: Handkerchief

Give children practice identifying beginning sounds as they play "Drop the Handkerchief."

Have a small group of children stand in a circle. The child who is "it" takes the handkerchief, walks around the outside of the circle, and drops the handkerchief behind one player. That player must name a word and then tell the letter that makes its beginning sound. If the player is correct, he or she then becomes the player to drop the handkerchief. To make the game more challenging, you may want to give a category for the words to be named, such as vegetables, plants, or animals.

340

FARMER IN THE DELL

When a "cat" takes a "cow," hi-ho the dairy-o!

Play a favorite singing game to help children practice beginning sounds.

Sing "Farmer in the Dell." Start with the traditional verse: "The farmer in the dell, the farmer in the dell, hi-ho the dairy-o, the farmer in the dell." For the second verse, begin by saying, "The farmer takes a cat." Have the child sing new verses, adding a new word beginning like the word *cat* each time. For example, the third verse might be "The cat takes a *cow*" and the fourth verse "The cow takes a *carrot*."

After the child has sung several verses, change to a new letter, such as *D* ("The farmer takes a *dog*"), and continue.

VISIT THE VET

341

It is time for your pet's annual check-up. Visit your veterinarian and have a learning experience.

A visit to the veterinarian can be a great learning experience for a child. It can help him or her to learn more about the family pet and the care that it needs.

On your ride to the doctor's office, discuss with the child what an animal doctor is called. (Answer: veterinarian.) Ask what letter is at the beginning of that word.

In the veterinarian's examining room, ask the child to name some things that he or she sees there—for example, a table, some cotton, a light, medicine, a stethoscope, and so on. Then, as you say a beginning letter, have him or her tell you the object that starts with that letter. Use the items that the child observed. While the veterinarian is examining your pet, ask him or her to tell the child what he or she is doing and why.

On your way home, talk about some of the *V* words that were encountered during the trip.

TONGUE TWISTERS

Marvin Moose made many more messy mud pies.
Fifty-five funny farmers found forty-four fancy forks.

342 ALPHABET EXPLORATION

The old neighborhood takes on a new look when it's explored the alphabetical way.

WHAT YOU'LL NEED: Paper, marker or pen

Send young adventurers out into the neighborhood on a search with an alphabet focus.

Choose a letter. Have the child walk through the neighborhood and look for all kinds of objects with that beginning letter. For example, the letter *R* might produce a robin, roses, ribbon, a rabbit, rain, rocks, runners, and a railroad track. After the walk, write down the names of the objects found as the child names them. Help him or her draw a map of the neighborhood, adding a picture of each item on the list in the location where it was spotted.

 ## BASKETBALL FUN 343

Basketball fans can learn letters and words while they play their favorite game.

WHAT YOU'LL NEED: Toy basketball hoop or empty ice cream container, small rubber ball

Children will enjoy playing basketball—and keeping score—in this beginning-sound game. If you do not have a toy basketball hoop, you can make one by cutting the bottom out of a large, empty ice cream container.

Hang the hoop on a door, and show the child how to score a basket with the rubber ball. Each time the child prepares to throw the ball, he or she must say a word that begins like *basketball* or like *fun*. The child receives one point for each basket he or she makes and one point for each correct word. Play until the child scores five points.

FUNNY FARM

344

Laugh and learn with this silly beginning-sound game.

WHAT YOU'LL NEED: Paper, marker or pen

Use children's love of tall tales to practice beginning sounds.

Start a Funny Farm story about an animal on your farm: "I have a gorilla who gulps guppies." Encourage the child to create another sentence. In each sentence, use a lot of words beginning with the initial sound in the animal's name. Take turns making up Funny Farm sentences. Then have the child draw a picture of the animals you have created.

345 # GROCERY STORE ADVENTURES

Take this shopping list to the grocery store on your next visit.

WHAT YOU'LL NEED: Grocery advertisements, paper, pen or pencil

Turn grocery shopping into a learning experience for the child with this activity.

Have the child make a shopping list from grocery circulars and advertisements. The child can do so by "reading" pictures and/or printed words and circle desired items. Help the child sound out and write down the names of the selected items.

On your next trip to the grocery store, the child can then shop for his or her items. As the item is found and placed in the cart, have the child cross it off the list. Emphasize the beginning sound of each item. Make sure the item selected is the same as the one on the list. The child will become more aware of categories of foods and will have to discriminate among the different brands of an item and match the food to the correct list item.

346 · · · · · · · NATURE COLLECTION · · · ·

See how many different nature items you can collect and label.

WHAT YOU'LL NEED: Small brown bag, collection of nature items (see below), shirt box, self-adhesive notes, marker or pen

Expand a child's environment by helping him or her collect nature objects, display and label those items in a box, and learn beginning sounds.

Go in your backyard or to the park, or take a nature walk with the child, and look for nature objects alphabetically. For example, you could say to the child, "Find something that begins like the word *bird*." (Possible solution: blueberries.) Next you might say, "Find something that begins like *sun*." (Possible solution: seeds.) Continue with other clues to find such items as leaves, a rock, an acorn, or a feather. As you find items, have the child put them in a small brown bag.

When your collecting is complete and you are inside your home, have the child place the collected nature items in a shirt box. Give the child a pad of self-adhesive notes and a marker or pen to write the beginning letter of each item and then place that label by the correct item.

Try this activity at different times of the year and see how the nature items vary.

RIDDLE TIME
– – – – – – – – – –
I have a comb, a beak, and two legs.

I live on the farm and I lay eggs.

(a hen)

LETTER LION

Make friends with a lion that only eats letters.

WHAT YOU'LL NEED: Large sheet of brown wrapping paper, marker or pen, blunt scissors, box, letter cards made from index cards

Younger children will enjoy practicing beginning sounds by feeding a hungry lion.

On brown wrapping paper, draw a large lion's head. Cut a large round hole for a mouth. Put the lion's head on a box with a hole cut in the position of the lion's mouth. You might also hang the lion on a door. In order to feed the lion, the child must take a letter card, identify the letter, and say a word that begins with the sound the letter stands for. If the child gives correct answers, he or she drops the card into the lion's mouth.

BEGINNING, MIDDLE, OR END?

348

Like the best stories, most words have a beginning, a middle, and an end.

WHAT YOU'LL NEED: Piece of poster board, blunt scissors, marker or pen, letter cards

In this activity, children who have mastered beginning sounds practice listening for letter sounds in other parts of a word.

Cut a piece of poster board approximately 18″ × 6″. Divide it into three sections. Choose a letter card. Say some words that have that letter at the beginning, middle, and end. For example, for the letter *S*, you might slowly say the words *syrup, messy,* and *bus.* Have the child place the letter card on the beginning, middle, or end section of the letter strip to indicate the *S* sound's position in each word. Select a new letter and repeat the activity.

SPIN AND WIN

▼▼▼▼▼▼▼▼▼▼▼▼▼▼▼▼▼▼▼▼▼▼▼▼▼▼▼▼▼▼▼

349

*Even phonics wizards will need some luck to win
this fast-moving game.*

WHAT YOU'LL NEED: Poster board, paper fastener, index cards, blunt scissors, six pictures of common items cut from an old magazine, glue or clear tape, marker or pen

This spinning game requires both luck and knowledge of beginning sounds.

On the poster board, draw a large circle and divide it into six sections. Write a letter on the edge of each section. Cut out a long spinner, and attach it to the center of the circle with a paper fastener. Next, make a set of six picture cards (pictures cut from old magazines glued or taped to index cards). Each card should show an object whose name begins with one of the letters on the circle. Shuffle the cards and put them in a stack.

To play the game, a player spins the spinner and takes the top picture card from the pile. If the name of the picture begins with the letter sound he or she has spun, the player keeps the picture. If not, the next player spins. Continue taking turns until all the picture cards have been won.

350  # PHONETIC FOOTBALL

*Colorful football cutouts help kids score
with beginning sounds.*

WHAT YOU'LL NEED: Construction paper, blunt scissors, marker or pen

Encourage sports lovers to practice beginning sounds.

Cut six football shapes out of construction paper. Print a different letter on each football. Place the footballs in a row. Have the child start at the left end of the row and say a word that begins with the sound of the letter on the football. Explain to the child that, to score a touchdown, he or she must reach the other end of the row by saying a word for each football's letter. Play again by adding new letters.

351 — A DAY AT THE RACES —

It could be a photo finish when kids who know beginning sounds play this board game.

WHAT YOU'LL NEED: Poster board or wrapping paper, marker or pen, letter cards made from index cards, die and markers from a board game

Try this race track board game to practice beginning sounds. First, draw a large oval race track on a poster board or a large sheet of wrapping paper. Write *Start* and *Finish* at the appropriate places. Mark the track with small squares, and place a letter card in each one. Place game markers at the beginning of the track.

Players take turns rolling the die and moving their markers along the track. When a player lands on a square, he or she must identify the letter and say a word that begins with the sound the letter stands for. If the player gives an incorrect answer, he or she goes back to *Start.* Play until someone reaches the *Finish* line.

ALPHABET CATEGORIES — 352

Pick a category, and see how many words you can come up with.

Here's a game that can be played in the car or whenever you have a few spare minutes.

Ask the child to help choose a category, such as animals, foods, or toys. The first player must name a member of the category whose name begins with the letter *A.* The next player names one whose name begins with the letter *B,* and so on.

You may need to give the child clues for some words (having several ABC picture books may be helpful). Also, explain to the child that it may be difficult or impossible to come up with words for some letters. If a child is forced to "pass" and no one else can think of a word that begins with that letter either, he or she can move on to the next letter of the alphabet.

WHERE CAN IT BE?

353

Need two grocery items of the same thing? This is the activity for you.

Grocery shopping can be unpleasant for a young child, but by involving him or her in the process, it can become more interesting .

Return to an aisle where you have already selected an item—for example, the cereal aisle. Ask the child to find another box of the same cereal. This is great when you need two of a certain item, although you can always put one of the boxes back on the shelf. In this activity, the child will need to focus on the label (picture and writing), the size, and the shape of the item in order to make a correct match. Be sure that when you select an item it is on a shelf at or below the child's eye level so he or she can reach it.

354

LETTER HOPSCOTCH

Hop to it, and enjoy a new way to play hopscotch.

WHAT YOU'LL NEED: Chalk, bean bag

Here's a letter game that's good for active children.

On a sidewalk or safe driveway, mark off a hopscotch game. Put a capital letter in each box as illustrated in the accompanying drawing. The child tosses the bean bag into letter square *A*, then hops over letter *A*, landing on each of the other hopscotch grid letters in succession. The child then turns around and hops into the letter squares in reverse order. From letter *B*, however, the child picks up the bean bag in letter square *A*, hops into that square, and then hops out of the grid.

On the next turn, the child throws the bean bag to letter *B* and hops from letter *A* to *C*, and so on, repeating the procedure as before. The child always hops over the box that has the bean bag in it, until picking up the bag on the return trip and hopping out of the grid.

SMART ART

355

Visiting an art museum with a child can be an enlightening experience on many different levels.

Expand a child's world—and practice beginning sounds—by visiting an art museum and studying the paintings and sculptures found there.

Select a particular gallery in the museum that you think the child would enjoy seeing. If a certain painting or sculpture attracts the child's attention, go to that piece of art. Look at it together, and have the child describe it to you. Ask him or her to find something in the painting that begins with a certain letter, or name a letter and ask the child to identify an object in the artwork that begins with that letter. Tell the child the name of the artist who created the artwork.

When you are at home or at the library, see if you can find a book about the child's favorite artist, or find a book that contains a photo of a painting the child likes, perhaps one seen at the museum.

356 # SWEATIN' TO THE ALPHABET

Time to exercise! Have the child help you with a new exercise routine.

Both you and the child will benefit from exercising together.

To develop a routine, ask the child to think of some ways to exercise. Give the child a letter, and have him or her think of an exercise move for that letter. For example, *B* could stand for *bend*, *J* for *jump*, *H* for *hop*, *T* for *touch toes*, *S* for *stretch*, and so on. Do the exercises together. Very active children—and their parents—can benefit greatly from this activity.

LETTER LINE

357

Using clothespins to learn beginning sounds keeps kids from getting out of line.

WHAT YOU'LL NEED: String, objects described below, index cards, marker or pen, plastic clothespins

Children can work on beginning sounds by hanging letter cards and objects from a line.

Stretch a piece of string across a secluded corner of the house, and secure it on both ends. Collect several objects that can be hung from the line, such as a sock, napkin, mitten, letter, paper plate, and towel. Next, make letter cards containing both the capital and lowercase forms of the beginning letter of each chosen item.

Have the child choose an object and hang it on the line. Then have him or her find the letter card that shows the beginning sound of the object's name and hang it next to the object. When the child has hung all the objects and matching letter cards along the line, have him or her name each object and the beginning sound of its name.

358

CAREERS FROM A TO Z

Consider careers—from acrobat to zoologist— in this alphabet game.

WHAT YOU'LL NEED: Large sheet of paper or poster board, marker or pen

Here's a project that relates to the question, "What do you want to be when you grow up?"

Help the child make a poster illustrating various careers. Begin with the letter *A,* and ask the child to think of a career whose name begins with that letter, such as *astronaut.* Have the child write the letter and draw a picture of an astronaut. Continue through the alphabet, skipping letters that don't work or do not bring an easy response.

359 GO FLY A KITE

The sky is clear. The wind is blowing. Go fly a kite on this beautiful, windy day.

WHAT YOU'LL NEED: Kite

Next time you look out the window and see that the wind is blowing and the leaves are moving, ask the child, "What is making the leaves blow?" (Answer: wind.) Have the child place a hand in front of his or her mouth, then ask him or her, "What do you feel on your hand when you say the word *wind?*" (Answer: wind.) Then say to the child, "I am thinking of something that needs wind to make it fly. It's a word that begins like *kitten*. What is it?" (Answer: a kite.)

Get a kite, go outside, and discuss how to fly it. Say to the child, "I am thinking of something that you will need to do to lift the kite in the air. This word begins like *race*. What is it?" (Answer: run.) Talk about other beginning-letter sounds involved in kite flying, such as *T* for tail, *S* for string, and *H* for high.

Now that the child knows how to fly a kite, have him or her face into the wind, put the kite on the ground, hold the string tight, and run. In just a matter of minutes, the kite will be flying high.

TONGUE TWISTERS

Jolly Jack the juggler jumped over Jean the jogging joker.

CAT AND MOUSE

360

Here's a chance for the child to feel like the "big cheese."

WHAT YOU'LL NEED: Letter cards

Here's a game that will challenge a child to move quickly and quietly.

Have the child imagine that he or she is a mouse and that you are a cat. The "mouse" must take the "cheese"—a letter card—without getting caught by the "cat."

Sit in a chair. Place a letter card on the floor behind you. Close your eyes, and wait for the child to take the card. If you hear him or her, say, "I hear a mouse." If you speak before the child has picked up the card, he or she must take your place on the chair, and you must try to take the card. If the child takes the card without getting caught, he or she must name a word that begins with the letter on the card. The child then keeps the card, a new card is laid down, and the game is repeated. The player who successfully takes the most cards wins.

361

ALPHABETICAL SHOPPING

From apples to zucchini, the grocery store has everything. What can you find?

WHAT YOU'LL NEED: Paper, pen or pencil

Try this alphabetical shopping activity. It may take some extra time.

Before going grocery shopping, ask the child to help you put your shopping list in alphabetical order. If the list is short and you don't mind doing a little extra walking, locate the items in the store in alphabetical order.

If your shopping list is long, shop as you normally do, but let the child cross off each item from the list as you locate it.

A apple
B butter
C cereal
D donuts
E eggs
F fish
G grapes
H hot dogs

ASPARAGUS TO ZUCCHINI

Plant an alphabet garden from asparagus to zucchini.

WHAT YOU'LL NEED: Vegetable seeds, pots and soil (if planting indoors), tape, Popsicle sticks, marker, paper

Planting a garden encourages a child to develop responsibility, especially if he or she agrees to water and care for the plants.

Take the child to the store to help select different vegetable seeds to plant in your garden. Ask the child, "What vegetable begins like the word *buy?*" (Answers: beans, beets, or broccoli.) Then have the child point to that vegetable's seed packet. Continue giving other beginning-sound clues for other vegetables. Purchase the seeds. If you don't have an outdoor garden, purchase some pots and soil to use for planting indoors.

On your trip home, discuss how you and the child will begin planting. Ask the child, "What vegetable did you select that begins with the letter *B* (or other letters, depending on which vegetables were selected)?"

At planting time, read the seed packet planting directions to the child, then have him or her tell you what steps are necessary for planting these seeds. After the seeds are planted, save the packet and tape or otherwise secure it to a Popsicle stick. Have the child write the beginning letter of that vegetable on the stick with a marker, then place this stick by the planted seeds.

Make a simple chart on which the child can place an X each day that the vegetables were cared for and watered. This encourages and reinforces responsibility on the part of the child.

Good luck with the garden, and enjoy eating those special vegetables.

363 ALLIGATORS TO ZEBRAS

Alligators, elephants, tigers, and zebras. What other animals are in the zoo?

Today is the day to visit the zoo. To prepare the child for this visit, think of an animal and the sound it makes as you are traveling to the zoo. Make this sound, and see if the child can identify it. Then have the child think of other animals and mimic their sounds.

When you arrive at the zoo, tell the child to look for animals that begin like the words *mom* (monkey), *ball* (bear), *ticket* (tiger), *zoo* (zebra), and *sign* (seal). As you are observing these and other animals, have the child listen for the sounds that each animal makes, then name the animal and say its beginning letter.

On your next visit to the library, or while on-line on your computer, locate pictures and information about some of the animals you saw at the zoo.

TONGUE TWISTERS

Now nurse Nancy needs nine new nifty necklaces.

364 PICTURE POCKETS

Poking through pockets produces plenty of practice with the letter P in this activity.

WHAT YOU'LL NEED: Purse with pockets, magazines, blunt scissors

This activity rewards children's search through a purse with pictures of objects beginning with the letter *P*.

Find an old purse or wallet with several pockets and compartments. Cut pictures from magazines of items beginning with *P*. Put a picture in each pocket of the purse. Instruct the child to find one picture at a time and name it. For an extra challenge, have the child find pictures of objects that begin with the letter *P* to put into the picture pockets.

COMICAL COMICS 365

Kids can have fun with phonics by focusing on the funnies.

WHAT YOU'LL NEED: Comic strip from newspaper, blunt scissors

Reading the comics is a great way to introduce children to newspapers.

Read several comic strips with the child. Point out simple words as you read. Have the child choose a favorite strip and tell it in his or her own words. Then cut out the strip, and cut the strip into its parts. Mix the pieces up. Have the child arrange the pieces in order and tell the story. Don't worry if the pieces are not in their original order, as long as the child tells the story in a logical way.

PRINTED ALPHABET

Below are the alphabet's letters in their common printed forms. Children are taught this "ball and stick" style in the primary grades, so it's important for parents to teach this style to their preschoolers.

Aa Bb Cc Dd Ee
Ff Gg Hh Ii Jj Kk
Ll Mm Nn Oo Pp
Qq Rr Ss Tt Uu Vv
Ww Xx Yy Zz

MOST COMMON WORDS

These are the 100 most commonly used words in the English language. Altogether they make up about 50 percent of all written language. Therefore, it is important that the child learn to recognize all of the words in this list, and eventually learn how to say, write, and define them.

1. the	21. at	41. there	61. some	81. my
2. of	22. be	42. use	62. her	82. than
3. and	23. this	43. an	63. would	83. first
4. a	24. have	44. each	64. make	84. water
5. to	25. from	45. which	65. like	85. been
6. in	26. or	46. she	66. him	86. called
7. is	27. one	47. do	67. into	87. who
8. you	28. had	48. how	68. time	88. oil
9. that	29. by	49. their	69. has	89. its
10. it	30. words	50. if	70. look	90. now
11. he	31. but	51. will	71. two	91. find
12. was	32. not	52. up	72. more	92. long
13. for	33. what	53. other	73. write	93. down
14. on	34. all	54. about	74. go	94. day
15. are	35. were	55. out	75. see	95. did
16. as	36. we	56. many	76. number	96. get
17. with	37. when	57. then	77. no	97. come
18. his	38. your	58. them	78. way	98. made
19. they	39. can	59. these	79. could	99. may
20. I	40. said	60. so	80. people	100. part

PHONOGRAMS

The following list contains some of the most commonly used phonograms (and the symbol representing the sound of the key vowel) in the English language. A phonogram is a series of letters that is consistantly used to form words. The child should study this list in order to learn the many different words derived from the same sounds.

-ace (ā)	-ain (ā)	game	-are (ā)	-eat (ē)	-ight (ī)	-ink (ĭ)	-old (ō)
face	gain	name	bare	beat	fight	link	bold
lace	main	same	care	feat	knight	pink	cold
race	pain	tame	dare	heat	light	rink	fold
brace	rain	blame	fare	meat	might	sink	hold
grace	brain	flame	rare	neat	night	wink	old
place	chain	frame	scare	peat	right	blink	sold
space	drain	shame	share	seat	tight	drink	told
	grain		spare	cheat	bright	think	
-ad (ă)	plain		square	treat	flight		**-ot (ŏ)**
bad	sprain	**-an (ă)**	stare	wheat		**-ip (ĭ)**	cot
dad	stain	ban			**-ill (ĭ)**	dip	got
fad	train	can	**-ave (ā)**	**-ell (ĕ)**	bill	hip	hot
had		man	cave	bell	fill	lip	lot
mad	**-ake (ā)**	pan	gave	sell	hill	rip	not
pad	bake	ran	rave	tell	ill	tip	spot
sad	cake	tan	save	well	will	chip	
glad	fake	van	wave	yell	drill	drip	**-ow (ou)**
	lake	bran	brave	shell	grill	flip	bow
-ail (ā)	make	plan	crave	smell	skill	ship	cow
bail	rake	than	shave	spell	still	skip	how
fail	take					trip	now
jail	wake	**-and (ă)**	**-eak (ē)**	**-ent (ĕ)**	**-ing (ĭ)**		brow
mail	brake	band	beak	bent	king	**-ock (ŏ)**	plow
nail	flake	hand	leak	dent	ring	dock	
pail	shake	land	peak	rent	sing	lock	**-ow (ō)**
rail	snake	sand	weak	sent	wing	knock	low
sail	stake	bland	sneak	tent	bring	rock	row
tail		gland	speak	vent	spring	sock	flow
snail	**-ame (ā)**	grand	squeak	went	string	block	show
trail	came	stand	streak	scent	swing	clock	slow
	fame	strand		spent	thing	flock	snow

INDEX